ARCTIC OCEAN
MONGOLIAN REPUBLIC
CHINA

Soviet Union

W. A. Douglas Jackson

Dr. W. A. Douglas Jackson is known internationally as a geographer and as an author of geographical articles on the Soviet Union. He is Professor of Geography at the University of Washington. Dr. Jackson has done post-graduate work at the University of Toronto, the University of Maryland, and the Russian Institute of Columbia University. He has been a fellow of the Harvard Russian Research Center, and has traveled extensively in the Soviet Union. Dr. Jackson's background of research and travel enables him to describe the land and people of the Soviet Union in a comprehensive and interesting manner.

Printed in the U. S. A. by offset lithography.

LIBRARY OF CONGRESS CATALOG CARD NUMBER: 62-8849

EDITORS AND ADVISORS

LIFE IN OTHER LANDS

CANADA
MEXICO
BRAZIL
SOUTH AMERICA
AUSTRALIA
JAPAN
CHINA
INDIA
SOVIET UNION
AFRICA

LIFE IN EUROPE

NORWAY
SWEDEN
THE BRITISH ISLES
THE NETHERLANDS
GERMANY
FRANCE
SWITZERLAND
AUSTRIA
ITALY
SPAIN

SOVIET UNION

W. A. Douglas Jackson

THE FIDELER COMPANY—GRAND RAPIDS, MICHIGAN

Grateful acknowledgment is made to the following for permission to use the illustrations found in this book:

Bernadine Bailey: Pages 73 and 100.
Camera Press-Pix: Pages 23, 25, 67, 121, and 130.
Charlotte Saikowski: Pages 19, 22, 101, 108, and 155.
Culver Pictures, Inc.: Page 36.
Clark: Pages 56, 136, 175, and 176.
Free Lance Photographers Guild, Inc.: Page 95.
Julien Bryan: Pages 32, 53, 70, 89, 94, and 157.
Keystone: Page 42.
Magnum: Pages 58, 153, 161, and 169.
Momsen: Pages 29, 159, and 167.
Panoramic Studios: Map on page 8.
Paramount Pictures: Page 174.
Paul's Photos: Pages 20, 55, 78, 83, 86, 88, 93, 99, 110, 151, and 156.
Pictorial Parade, Inc.: Pages 63, 152, 168, and 179.
Pix, Inc.: Pages 9 and 68.
Radio Times Hulton Picture Library – London, England: Pages 38, 40, 43, 45, 49, 50, 51, and 54.
Soviet Information Bureau – Moscow, U.S.S.R.: Pages 14, 16, 31, 33, 46, 60, 76, 77, 85, 104, 112, 114, 116, 118, 119, 125, 131, 160, 163, 165, 166, and 178.
Sovfoto: Pages 12, 17, 18, 26, 44, 47, 64, 65, 71, 74, 75, 80, 82, 96, 97, 98, 102, 103, 105, 107, 111, 113, 115, 122, 123, 127, 133, 135, 143, 146, 148, 158, 164, 171, 172, and 184.
Stuart Phillips: Pages 173 and 177.
TASS – Moscow, U.S.S.R.: Pages 3, 15, 21, 24, 30, 39, 57, 66, 79, 90, 129, 137, 139, 140, 141, 142, 145, 149, 154, 180, 181, and 183.
Toni McElrath: Page 72.

TO THE TEACHER

There Are Only Two Effective Ways to Study Geography

There are only two effective ways for children to form the clear mental images needed to understand the geography of the Soviet Union. One is to take geography field trips through this country. The other is to use in the classroom many good geography pictures accompanied by vivid text.

A Better Way to Study The Soviet Union in Your Classroom

Arouse Interest and Help Students Think. Use five to ten copies of the *Soviet Union* textbook and one copy of the *Soviet Union* portfolio of Classroom Pictures (loose-leaf edition of the book) to interest your students in exploring the Soviet Union.

Keep Children Thinking. Divide the class into committees, each of which will seek answers to such questions as:

. . . What are the land and climate of the Soviet Union like?
. . . What are the people of the Soviet Union like?
. . . How do the people of the Soviet Union make a living?
(See list of chapters in this book.)

For its research work, let each committee use traditional textbooks and one or more copies of the *Soviet Union* textbook, plus those chapters and pictures from the *Soviet Union* portfolio that relate to the topic the committee is investigating.

When research has been completed, let each committee present its most important findings to the class. The committee should be questioned by the rest of the class and the teacher.

Give Every Child a Chance to Think and Learn. This *Soviet Union* textbook is designed for use on three reading ability levels. (See next page.) When you use five to ten copies of the *Soviet Union* textbook and the matching portfolio of Classroom Pictures in the manner described above, you give every child a chance to think and learn. Slow learners, children with average abilities, and students with superior minds are able to find answers to their questions and to form vivid mental images that are necessary for understanding the geography of the Soviet Union.

How to Meet the Learning Needs of Every Child

The editors of this book believe that the secret of successful learning lies in motivating the student to *think.* This fundamental principle has been effectively stated by John Dewey in his book *Democracy and Education:* "The sole path to enduring improvement in the methods of instruction and learning consists in centering upon the conditions which exact, promote, and test thinking. Thinking *is* the method of intelligent learning; of learning that employs and rewards the mind." Our great need is to lead students to think purposefully.

Purpose and Interest

Purpose and interest are the most important elements of thinking. To expect students to read and think about geography without first helping them find a purpose, or an interest, is to invite their failure. The first step in teaching geography should be to create a highly challenging environment that will arouse the natural curiosity of the students. The teacher may create this environment with the help of the proper learning aids. A good filmstrip or large pin-up-board pictures will let all the students of the class see vivid views of life in the Soviet Union. Good geography pictures are a powerful aid for creating interest and developing purpose on the part of the student. The clear, lighted pictures in a good filmstrip that shows vivid, fascinating views of the Soviet Union and its people appeal to every student's natural curiosity. If a filmstrip or a collection of good geography pictures about the Soviet Union is not available, the teacher can group the students in such a way that the entire class may share most effectively all of the copies of this textbook that are in the classroom. If the attention of each member of the class is centered on the same picture at the same time, the students as a group can enjoy visual experiences that are almost as satisfactory as those made possible by a filmstrip or bulletin board display.

Successful motivation will bring forth a number of questions to which the class will want to find answers. These questions should be recorded, discussed, and revised by the group. Those that offer a true challenge to the students' efforts open the way for a profitable study of the Soviet Union.

[A portfolio of geography pictures of the Soviet Union size 9-1/4" x 12-3/16" has been published for use with this book and other geography textbooks. It may be secured from Informative Classroom Picture Publishers, Grand Rapids 2, Michigan. (*Soviet Union*—48 plates—$3.95.) Sixteen chapters of loose-leaf text are included for reference use by the students.]

Three Levels of Reading Ability

This book is designed for use on three ability levels to help the teacher provide for the great differences in reading ability found in the average class. It provides a means for purposeful investigation and purposeful reading by students on each of the following ability levels:

1 — A few of the students will read purposefully only the pictures, some of the maps, and many of the captions.

2 — Most of the students will read the pictures and the captions, the maps, and much of the text.

3 — Some will read all of the text, the pictures and their captions, and the maps.

In each class there will be a few students who will read the book most effectively on the first level only. Each of these students urgently needs a copy of the book for his individual use. The challenging pictures and captions in each chapter make it possible for these students to share many important learning experiences. The teacher will be pleased to observe how much essential information is gained and what thought-provoking experiences are shared by these students, even though they are reading at the first level.

In the average geography class in which the Soviet Union is studied, nearly every student will be able to use the book successfully. At various times, as the study progresses, each student will read at one or more of these ability levels. All will make the same trip through the Soviet Union and will gain valuable experiences in geography. As a result, they will be able to participate more effectively in group discussion and in group activity, based on an understanding of the important features of the Soviet Union.

How Many Copies Are Needed?

Each teacher must answer the question: "How many copies of this book are needed for my class?" Each teacher must personally assume responsibility for securing the learning aids that will enable his students to learn successfully. If the class is divided into committees, as described on the preceding page, as few as five books and one portfolio can effectively serve a class of thirty students.

The Editors

CONTENTS

Chapter		Page
	SOME THINGS TO KNOW BEFORE YOU READ THIS BOOK	8
I.	THE LAND	13
II.	THE CLIMATE	25
III.	EARLY HISTORY	34
IV.	MODERN HISTORY	46
V.	GOVERNMENT	56
VI.	THE PEOPLE	68
VII.	FARMING AND GRAZING	83
VIII.	A VISIT TO A COLLECTIVE FARM VILLAGE	95
IX.	NATURAL RESOURCES	104
X.	INDUSTRY	115
XI.	TRANSPORTATION AND COMMUNICATION	127
XII.	CITIES	137
XIII.	SPORTS AND RECREATION	152
XIV.	EDUCATION	160
XV.	ARTS OF THE PAST	169
XVI.	ART TODAY IN THE SOVIET UNION	178
	GLOSSARY	185
	INDEX	191
	LIST OF MAPS	192

SOME THINGS TO KNOW BEFORE YOU READ THIS BOOK

Two giant neighbors. The two most powerful nations in the world are shown on the map above. One is the United States of America. The other is the Union of Soviet Socialist Republics, which we also call the Soviet Union. At one place these two giant neighbors are separated by only two and one-half miles of water.

A country of little freedom. The people of the Soviet Union do not have many of the freedoms that you and I consider important. They are not permitted to travel wherever they please or to read many books and magazines from other countries. If they disapprove of the way their government is run, they cannot even vote to put their leaders out of power.

The leaders of the Soviet Union are members of the Communist Party. The Party believes that individual people should not own farms, factories, or mines. All the natural resources and industries in the Soviet Union are owned by the government. The government decides what crops the farms are to produce, what goods the factories are to make, and what jobs the people are to hold.

Under the Communists, the Soviet Union has become a powerful industrial nation. It plans to overtake the United States. The people of the Soviet Union have been forced to go without many things in order that their country might make this progress.

A country of great ambitions. The leaders of the Soviet Union believe that someday all the world's nations will have Communist governments. To bring this about, they have forced neighboring countries to establish governments of this kind. They encourage Communists in countries that are still free to seize control of the governments. In many places they have been successful. Today more than one third of the world's people live under communism.

A country we must learn about. We must learn about the Soviet Union in order to guard our freedoms and to strengthen our democratic form of government. When we compare our lives with those of the Soviet people, we will realize how important our freedoms are. When we understand the ambitions of the Communist leaders and know what they are doing to carry out their aims, we will work harder to keep our nation strong.

Visitors to Lenin's tomb. Lenin was an important Communist leader.

SPITSBERGEN
NORWAY
SWEDEN
FINLAND
DENMARK
NETH.
BELGIUM
GERMANY
CZECHOSLOVAKIA
POLAND
HUNGARY
ROMANIA
BALTIC SEA
BARENTS SEA
WHITE SEA
G. OF FINLAND
ARCT
R.S.F.S.R.
LITHUANIAN S.S.R.
LATVIAN S.S.R.
ESTONIAN S.S.R.
BELORUSSIAN S.S.R.
UKRAINIAN S.S.R.
MOLDAVIAN S.S.R.
Leningrad
Moscow
Kiev
Kharkov
Donetsk
Gorki
Kuibyshev
Sverdlovsk
Novosibirsk
Tashkent
Baku
Dnieper R.
Moskva R.
Volga R.
Oka R.
Don R.
Kama R.
Belaya R.
Ob R.
Irtysh R.
Syr Darya
Amu Darya
Ili R.
CRIMEA
BLACK SEA
CASPIAN SEA
Aral Sea
L. Balkhash
RUSSIAN SOVIET
URAL MOUNTAINS
WEST SIBERIAN PLAIN
Arctic Circle
CAUCASUS MTS.
GEORGIAN S.S.R.
ARMENIAN S.S.R.
AZERBAIJAN S.S.R.
KAZAKH S.S.R.
TURKMEN S.S.R.
UZBEK S.S.R.
KIRGHIZ S.S.R.
TADZHIK S.S.R.
TIEN SHAN MTS.
PAMIR MTS.
TURKEY
IRAQ
IRAN
AFGHANISTAN
CH

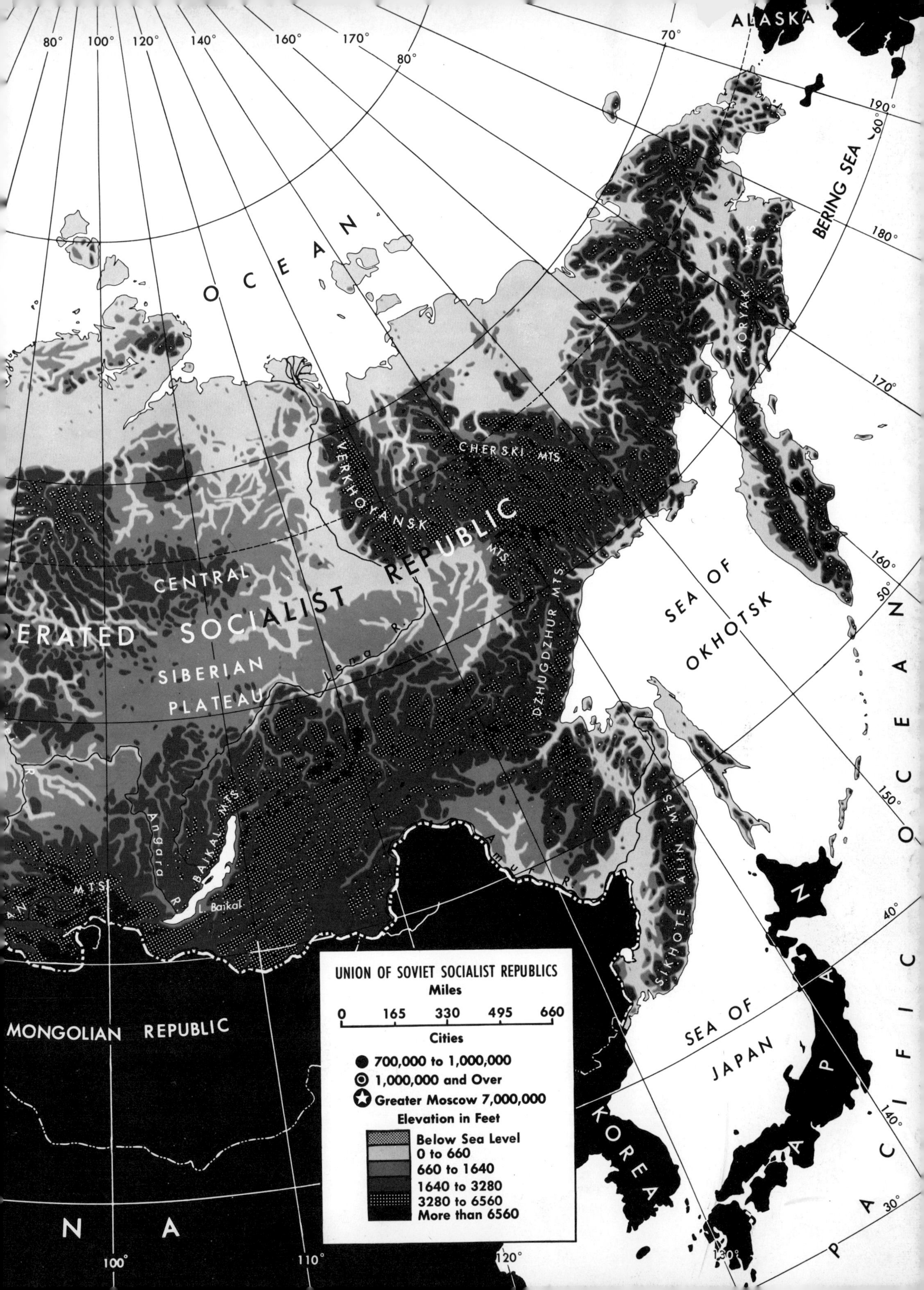

ALASKA
BERING SEA
OCEAN
CHERSKI MTS.
VERKHOYANSK MTS.
KORYAK MTS.
SEA OF OKHOTSK
DZHUGDZHUR MTS.
ERATED SOCIALIST REPUBLIC
CENTRAL SIBERIAN PLATEAU
Lena R.
Angara R.
BAIKAL MTS.
L. Baikal
Amur R.
SIKHOTE ALIN MTS.
SEA OF JAPAN
KOREA
JAPAN
PACIFIC OCEAN
MONGOLIAN REPUBLIC
N A
UNION OF SOVIET SOCIALIST REPUBLICS
Miles
0 165 330 495 660
Cities
700,000 to 1,000,000
1,000,000 and Over
Greater Moscow 7,000,000
Elevation in Feet
Below Sea Level
0 to 660
660 to 1640
1640 to 3280
3280 to 6560
More than 6560

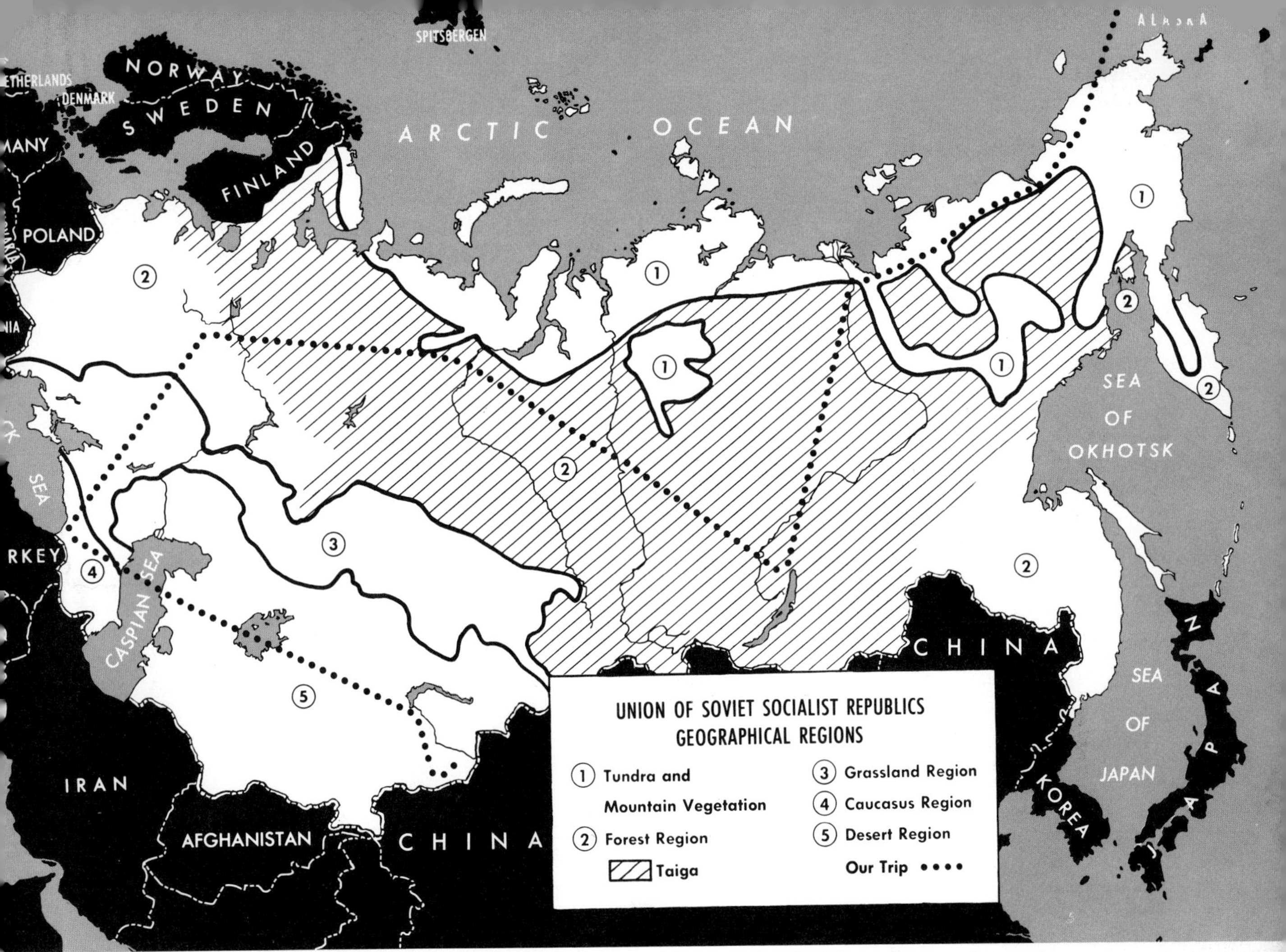

The Soviet Union is the largest country in the world. It is divided into five main regions.

CHAPTER ONE
THE LAND

The Soviet Union is the largest country on earth. It is nearly two and one-half times the size of the United States. (See map on page 8.) From east to west, this enormous country stretches six thousand miles. The western part lies in Europe. The eastern part covers the northern half of Asia. These two parts are separated by a low range of mountains called the Urals. (See map on pages 10 and 11.) Except for the Urals, and the highlands in the southern and eastern sections of the country, the land consists of a wide plain.

* Please see glossary, page 185.

Farmlands in Siberia. The northern part of Asia, which stretches from the Ural Mountains to the Pacific Ocean, is called Siberia.

The tundra stretches along the Arctic coast. It is a bleak region of plains and low hills.

The Soviet Union is partly bordered by great oceans and seas. (See map on pages 10 and 11.) To the north lies the icy Arctic Ocean. To the east are the Bering Sea, the Sea of Okhotsk, and the Sea of Japan. These seas are arms of the Pacific Ocean. Along part of the western border stretches the Baltic Sea, and far to the south lie the Black and Caspian seas.

The map on page 13 shows us that the Soviet Union is divided into five different regions. To learn what each of these is like, let us take an airplane trip across the country. We will board our plane in Alaska and follow the route shown on this map.

The tundra. The first region we see when we cross the northern coast of the Soviet Union is the lonely, treeless tundra. (See map on page 13.) As our plane flies westward across the tundra, we notice low hills and mile after mile of level, marshy plains. Snow and ice blanket the ground here in places for many months each year. It is July now, however. The countryside is covered with mosses, lichens,* and tufts of grass. Here and there in sheltered spots along the rivers are clumps of low bushes.

After flying westward across the tundra for about thirteen hundred miles, we come to the Lena River. (See map on page 11.) When we fly southward along this great waterway, we see more and more bushes and trees. Our pilot tells us that we are leaving the tundra and entering the forest region.

The Lena River flows through the forest region. This vast region covers about half the country.

The forest region. The map on page 13 shows us that the forest region stretches in a wide belt from the Pacific coast to the northwestern border of the country. It covers about one half of the Soviet Union.

As we follow the Lena River into the forest region, we notice that almost all the trees below us are evergreens. Trees which lose their leaves in winter grow mainly at the eastern and western ends of the forest region. The land in between is covered with evergreens. This evergreen forest is called the taiga. (See map on page 13.)

Flying over the taiga. The evergreen forest of the Soviet Union is called the taiga.

Lake Baikal is the deepest lake in the world. It is located in central Siberia.

There are many highlands in the eastern part of the forest region. The great tableland across which we are now flying is called the Central Siberian Plateau. (See map on page 11.) As we travel southward over this plateau, we notice that it is cut by deep river valleys.

When we reach the southern edge of the plateau, mountains loom up in front of us. Their lower slopes are covered with grass. Green forests grow on the higher slopes. In these mountains we see a long, narrow body of water. This is Lake Baikal, the deepest lake in the world. (See map on page 11.)

In the Ural Mountains. The Belaya River winds through these low, wooded mountains.

To see the rest of the forest region, we fly northwestward from Lake Baikal. After we cross the Yenisei River, we notice that the land becomes very flat and swampy. (See map on page 10.) We continue to fly over swampy forests for almost eight hundred miles until we cross another great river, called the Ob. Soon we see the low, wooded slopes of the Ural Mountains ahead of us. There are many industrial towns in these mountains, for rich deposits of iron and other ores are found here.

From the Ural Mountains to the western border of the Soviet Union stretches a wide plain. As we fly westward over this plain, we notice that the forest has been cleared in many places, and fields of crops have been planted. Farming villages and busy industrial cities dot the countryside. Many freight barges and cargo ships travel along the wide Volga River, which flows across the plain. Not far from the Volga River we see the capital city, Moscow. (See map on page 10.)

When we fly southward from Moscow, we see fewer and fewer trees. Our pilot tells us that we are leaving the forest region and entering the grassland region of the Soviet Union. (See map on page 13.)

In the western part of the forest region are many farm villages and cities.

The grassland region. The Russians* call the grassland region the steppe. As we fly over the steppe, we see huge fields of wheat and other crops. Trees grow only near villages and along the banks of rivers.

Near the southern edge of the steppe lie the Black Sea and the Caspian Sea. Between these two seas rises a high range of mountains called the Caucasus Mountains. As we approach these snow-covered peaks, we leave the steppe behind us and enter the Caucasus region. (See map on page 13.)

Vast fields of grain cover much of the grassland region. This region is called the steppe.

The rugged Caucasus Mountains lie between the Caspian Sea and the Black Sea.

The Caucasus region. The Caucasus Mountains and the land that lies beyond them form the smallest region in the Soviet Union. When we fly across it, we notice that the countryside differs greatly from place to place. The towering peaks of the Caucasus Mountains are covered with massive glaciers and sparkling snow. Below the snow line are many grassy meadows where shepherds are tending flocks of sheep. The lower slopes of the mountains are covered with trees.

Along the Black Sea coast. Tea bushes and vineyards grow on sheltered slopes near the Black Sea.

The land south of these mountains is called Transcaucasia, which means "across the Caucasus." It is partly bordered on the south by more mountain ranges, which continue southward into the neighboring countries of Iran and Turkey. Between these ranges and the Caucasus Mountains lies a plateau. It slopes gradually down to the Black Sea on the west and to the Caspian Sea on the east. (See map on page 10.) The slopes that face the Black Sea are green with tea bushes, vineyards, and forests. However, when we turn and fly eastward toward the Caspian, we notice that parts of the countryside are dry and brown.

The desert region. We cross the Caspian Sea to the desert region. (See map on page 13.) This region stretches farther south than any other part of the Soviet Union. Most of the land here is flat. However, we often see sand that has been piled in high ridges by the wind. Now our plane crosses the shallow Aral Sea. About six hundred miles farther to the east we come to Lake Balkhash. Strangely enough, this shallow lake is salty only at its eastern end. The Ili River brings fresh water to its western end.

We turn now and fly toward the lofty mountains that lie along most of the southern border of the desert region. Near the foot of the mountains are bright-green fields of crops. Streams from the mountains provide water for these farmlands.

The desert region lies east of the Caspian Sea. It reaches farther south than any other region.

Our plane rises steeply now so that we may get a better view of the rugged mountain peaks. Some of them tower more than four miles above sea level. They are covered with snow throughout the year. Beyond these mountains lie the countries of Afghanistan and China. We will not visit them, however, for we still have much to see in the Soviet Union.

DO YOU KNOW

1. How does the Soviet Union compare in size with other countries? In what two continents is it located?
2. On the map on page 13, find the five regions of the Soviet Union. Tell what each region is like.
3. Where are the Soviet Union's mountains and lowlands?

High mountains tower along most of the southern border of the desert region.

Springtime in Soviet Central Asia.* Spring and fall are short in most parts of the Soviet Union.

CHAPTER TWO
THE CLIMATE

If we lived in the Soviet Union for a year, we would find a great difference between summer and winter weather. Summer days would be hot in most places we visited. In winter, however, we

* Please see glossary, page 185.

Horse-drawn sleighs. Snow blankets the ground for many months in most of the Soviet Union.

could travel by sleigh in many parts of the country, for the ground would be covered with snow. These two seasons would be separated by a very short spring and fall.

The map on pages 10 and 11 shows us why the Soviet Union has this kind of climate. We can see that much of this enormous country is far away from any large body of water. For this reason, very little of the land is cooled in summer or warmed in winter by mild ocean breezes. The map also shows that lowlands cover much of the country. Because these lowlands are not sheltered by mountains, they are swept in summer by hot winds and in winter by icy storms.

When we look at the Soviet Union on the map on page 8, we see another important reason why most of the country has long, bitterly cold winters. It lies much closer to the North Pole than the United States does.

Of course, there are some differences in climate throughout the Soviet Union. Let's learn what they are.

Climate in the tundra. Imagine that it is summer and we are standing on a marshy plain in the tundra. (See map on page 13.) The ground is very wet. Our guide explains that a frozen layer of soil beneath the surface of the ground keeps the melted snow from soaking into the earth. This frozen soil is called permafrost. We do not see trees here, for summers this far north are too short and cool for them to grow.

Though it is midnight, the sun is still shining. During this season, the northern part of the earth is tipped toward the sun, and lands north of the Arctic Circle* have continuous daylight for many weeks.

In winter the tundra looks very different. Then, the northern part of the earth is tipped away from the sun, and the sky is dark for many weeks. Snow blankets the ground in many places, and a great sheet of ice covers the Arctic Ocean.

Only at the far western tip of the tundra do the waters along the coast remain unfrozen in winter. A warm ocean current called the North Atlantic Drift brings milder winter temperatures to this part of the tundra.

Climate in the forest region. Now we are traveling across the great forest belt that covers about one half of the Soviet Union. (See map on page 13.) In the western part of this region, we notice that the trees have been cut in many places and the countryside is dotted with farms and cities. One reason why many people make their homes here is that the winters are not so bitterly cold. Even though ice and snow cover the ground for many months, the temperature does not fall too low for trees which lose their leaves in winter to live. Winds from the Atlantic Ocean bring these milder winter temperatures. This part of the Soviet Union is closer to the Atlantic than any other part of the country. These westerly winds also bring enough moisture for crops to grow well here during the warm summer days.

The central part of the forest region is too far away from the Atlantic to be influenced by mild ocean winds. Summers here are very warm. Although winters are sunny, they are so bitterly cold that only hardy evergreen trees grow well. Rivers remain frozen for more than five months each year. The world's coldest temperatures have been recorded in parts of the forest region that lie in Siberia.*

Rainfall in the Soviet Union varies from place to place. Much of the country is quite dry.

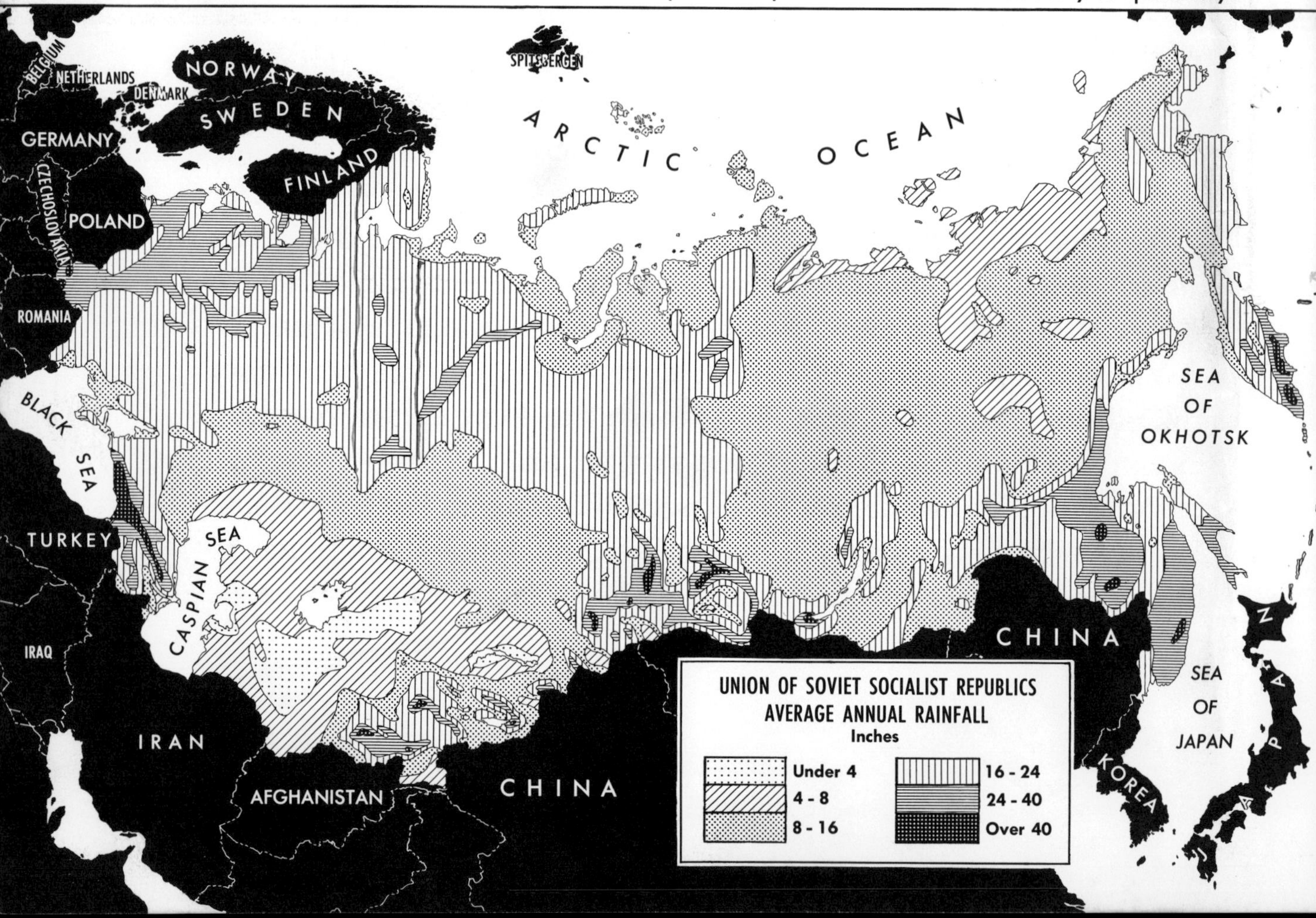

Summer in the Ukraine. Summers are hot throughout most of the Soviet Union.

Climate in the grasslands. Imagine now that we are in the wide grasslands that lie south of the forest region. (See map on page 13.) The summer air feels hot. A dry breeze rustles through the vast wheat fields that surround us. Less rain falls here than in the forest region, for the winds that come from the distant Atlantic Ocean have lost most of their moisture on their long journey.

The southern and eastern parts of the grasslands are drier than the northwestern part. Hot, dry winds often blow here in summer. When this happens, crops turn brown and die.

In winter, icy winds from the north blow across the grasslands. Winter is as cold here as it is in the forest region. Strong winds blow the snow across the frozen earth and pile it into drifts.

Climate in the desert. Southeast of the grasslands we come to the dusty, bleak desert. (See map on page 13.) Damp ocean winds do not reach this desolate region. It is too far from the Atlantic Ocean, and high mountains block the winds from the Indian Ocean to the south. The dry winds that do blow here bring less than eight inches of rain a year. Summer days in the desert are very hot. At night, however, the air quickly loses its heat. Winters are cold except in protected mountain valleys in the south.

Climate of the high mountains. Now we are climbing a high peak in the Caucasus Mountains, west of the desert. (See map on page 10.) The higher we go, the cooler the air becomes. Soon it is too cold for trees and bushes to grow. This high above sea level, the temperature is always so cold that snow stays on the ground

The desert receives less than eight inches of rainfall yearly. Summer days are hot and nights are cold.

A camp in the Caucasus Mountains. High in the mountains the climate is cool even in midsummer.

throughout the year. If we climbed the other high mountains in the Soviet Union, we would find this same kind of climate.

The vacation lands of the south. When we climb down the southwestern slopes of the Caucasus Mountains, we come to the shores of the Black Sea. The countryside is so fresh and green that we know much rain falls here. Because we see palm trees, we know also that the winter climate is very mild. We are not surprised to learn that people from many parts of the country spend their vacations in this area.

The high Caucasus Mountains that lie behind us and the Black Sea that stretches out before us are responsible for this mild,

A rainy winter day in Crimea. Mountains shelter this region from cold winter winds.

rainy climate. Moisture-filled winds from the sea bring the heavy rain that falls here. In winter the mountains shelter the land from icy northern gales.

Northwest of this coastal region lies another very popular vacation land. This is on the tip of Crimea, a peninsula which extends into the Black Sea. (See map on page 10.) Sheltering mountains help to give this area a mild winter climate, and sea breezes cool the summer air.

Climate on the far Pacific coast. To make our last visit, we must travel thousands of miles eastward to the Pacific coast of the Soviet Union. (See map on page 11.) Though it is midsummer, we notice that the air here is foggy and cool. It rains frequently during our visit. Moisture-filled winds from the sea bring this damp summer weather. These winds are cooled as they blow across a cold ocean current that flows southward along the Pacific coast of the Soviet Union. This causes them to lose their moisture along the coast in the form of rain. They lose still more moisture when they blow against the mountains along the coast.

If we visited the Pacific coast in winter, we would find the weather dry and cold. The winds that blow here at that season come from the north and northwest. They are so dry that they bring little snow. However, it is so cold that the snow which falls remains on the ground.

DO YOU KNOW

1. Describe the summers and winters in most of the Soviet Union. Give three reasons why the Soviet Union has this climate.
2. Explain why the ground is wet and swampy in the tundra during the summer.
3. What part of the country has mild winters?
4. On the map on page 28, locate the areas of heaviest rainfall.

Reindeer sleds near the Pacific coast. Winters here are cold, and summers are cool and rainy.

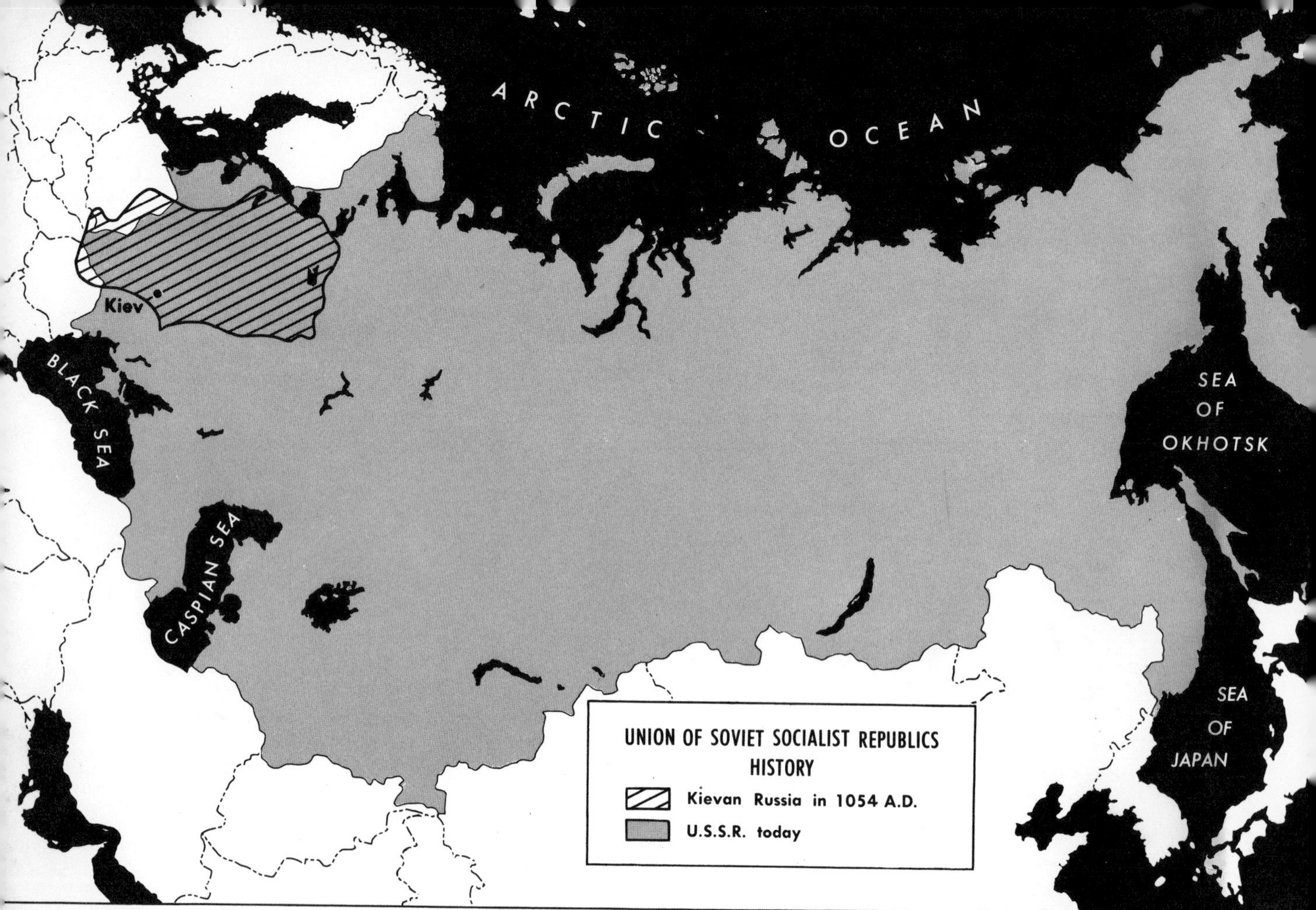

Kiev was the capital of early Russia. Vikings from the north helped to form this nation.

CHAPTER THREE

EARLY HISTORY

Early people. At the time that Christ was born, different groups of people were living in the vast land we now call the Soviet Union. In the southern grasslands were wandering tribesmen who lived in huts made of felt, which they carried from place to place. Farther north, in the forests, were primitive hunters and fishermen. Near what are now the western borders of the Soviet Union lived small groups of farmers. They were called Slavs.

Slavs move eastward and build towns. In the sixth and seventh centuries, many Slavs began to move eastward. Some traveled deep into the forests to make their homes. Others settled on the banks of the great Dnieper River. This waterway is part of a chain of rivers and lakes that leads from the Baltic Sea to the Black Sea. (See map on page 10.) Traders from northern Europe shipped their goods down this water route to a great city called Constantinople. The Slavs established trading towns along these rivers. These towns were like independent little countries with their own governments.

Seamen from the north unite the towns and form a nation. In the ninth century, daring sea warriors from Norway, Sweden, and Denmark began to sail along the rivers of Europe in search of riches. These were the Vikings. When they came to the Slavs' trading towns, many of them stayed there to live. In time, a Viking prince became the ruler of Kiev, the most important trading town. (See map on opposite page.) The princes of Kiev gained control of other towns. Their city became the capital of a large kingdom, which we call Kievan Russia.

Each year, traders from Kiev took boatloads of honey, furs, and wax to markets in the city of Constantinople. On their visits to this rich and beautiful city, they learned a great deal about art and building. They also learned about Christ. In 988 A.D., the Orthodox Eastern* form of Christianity practiced in Constantinople became the official religion of Kievan Russia.

Fierce horsemen from Asia conquer Kievan Russia. In the thirteenth century, fierce bands of warriors on horseback rode out of eastern Asia into Kievan Russia. These invaders, called Mongols, burned buildings and robbed and killed many people. In 1240, they captured Kiev. To escape the invaders, many people fled into the forests. For about the next 250 years, the Mongols controlled the country.

The invaders lose their power. Many of the people who fled into the forests settled near a wooden fortress overlooking the Moskva River. As time went on, this settlement grew into the city of Moscow. The princes of Moscow and the Mongols fought many battles. Finally the invaders lost their power.

The princes of Moscow become the rulers of Russia. The princes of Moscow became so powerful that they were able to gain control of the other towns around them. In time they formed a strong country with Moscow as its capital. This country came to be known as Russia. In 1547 the Russian ruler Ivan IV was crowned "tsar,"

The Mongols attacking Kiev. In the thirteenth century, Mongol invaders overran the country.

Ivan the Terrible was the first Russian ruler to be crowned "tsar," which means emperor.

which means emperor. Tsar Ivan added vast territories to Russia and ruthlessly destroyed people who opposed his power. He was such a harsh and powerful ruler that he is remembered as Ivan the Terrible.

Russia was almost destroyed after Tsar Ivan's death, for the rulers who followed him were very weak. The Russians were so busy quarreling among themselves that the neighboring country of Poland nearly gained control of their government. In 1613, however, the Russian people held a great assembly in Moscow and elected Michael Romanov to be their tsar. The Romanov family ruled Russia for the next 304 years.

Peter the Great studying shipbuilding. This ruler brought modern ways to Russia.

Peter the Great brings new ways to Russia. In 1697, a member of the Romanov family strode into a shipyard in Holland. The shipbuilders who saw this tall, strong man in workmen's clothing did not dream that he was Peter I, the tsar of Russia. Peter had come to Holland to learn modern methods of shipbuilding and other skills. He wanted to make his country more like the modern nations of western Europe. This would be difficult, for Russia was very backward. She had no navy, her army was old-fashioned, and very few of her people were educated.

Peter often used cruel methods to bring changes to his country. By the time he died, however, Russia was very different. Roads, canals, factories, and schools had been built. Even the capital had been moved from Moscow to a new city named St. Petersburg. Peter built this beautiful city on land along the Gulf of Finland, an arm of the Baltic Sea. He won this land in war from the nearby kingdom of Sweden.

Other nations begin to respect Russia. Some of Peter's changes made other countries in Europe respect Russia more. Until St. Petersburg was built, Russia had never had a seaport from which to trade easily with the countries of western Europe. This seaport made Russia a more important country.

Catherine the Great, who came to the throne in 1762, made other nations respect Russia even more. During her rule, the

A statue of Peter the Great in Leningrad. When Peter built this city he named it St. Petersburg.

Russians gained large territories from Turkey and Poland along the southern and western borders of the country.

In 1812 another event took place which increased Russia's reputation as a powerful nation. Several years earlier Napoleon, the

Catherine the Great. During her rule, Russia gained large territories from Turkey and Poland.

emperor of France, had set out to conquer all of Europe. He won victory after victory until he invaded Russia in 1812. To prevent the invading army from finding food or shelter, the Russians destroyed their own crops and burned the city of Moscow. Napoleon's soldiers were hungry and many of them froze to death during the cold winter months they spent in Russia. Only a small part of the army lived to return home. Russia received great praise in Europe for Napoleon's defeat.

Russia seeks new territories. The Russians wanted to become still more powerful. In 1821, the Tsar of Russia tried to claim the land along the Pacific coast of North America almost as far south as the state of Washington. The United States objected, so he changed his mind and claimed only Alaska. Later, this land was sold to the United States. The Russians also fought the neighboring countries of Persia* and Turkey for lands lying south of the high Caucasus Mountains.

Most of all, the Russians wanted to control two narrow sea passages called the Bosporus and the Dardanelles, through which they could send ships from the Black Sea to the Mediterranean Sea. These passageways were controlled by Turkey. In 1853, Russia invaded some of Turkey's possessions, mainly to gain control of the Bosporus and the Dardanelles. The next year, however, England and France, which were allies of Turkey, declared war on Russia. Together, with the kingdom of Sardinia, they defeated the Russians. This struggle was known as the Crimean War.

The Russians' defeat in the Crimean War did not discourage them from seeking new lands. In 1858 they took from China a large territory along the Pacific coast. Russian troops conquered, one after another, the small nations along the southern border of the country. Over the years, the tribes who lived in Siberia had been

Farm workers in Russia were very poor. Until they were freed in 1861, they worked as serfs.

conquered, too. Now the Russian Empire stretched from the Baltic Sea eastward to the Pacific and from the icy Arctic southward to the mountains in the heart of Asia.

Many people in Russia are dissatisfied. During the time that Russian armies were conquering new lands, Russian farm workers were living almost like slaves. These people, called serfs, worked on estates owned by nobles or by the royal family. The serfs were very poor, but they were not permitted to leave the estates and look for other jobs.

Other Russians were dissatisfied because they had no part in governing themselves. The tsars, with the help of their advisers, made all the laws. Newspapers and books were carefully censored* so that nothing would be printed of which the government did not approve. The rulers kept a strong force of secret police to spy on the people. No one was allowed to complain in public, so small groups of people began to meet secretly to discuss ways of reforming or overthrowing the government.

Tsar Alexander II, who came to the throne in 1855, made some changes, but they were not enough. In 1861, he passed a law freeing the serfs and permitting them to have farms. These farms were usually too small to make a living on, however, so most of the farm workers, or peasants,* were as poor and wretched as before. In 1881, a man belonging to one of the secret revolutionary groups killed Alexander with a bomb. The tsars who followed him were far more strict than he had been.

In 1905, workmen throughout Russia left their jobs and refused to come back until the government made some changes. Railroads,

Alexander II was killed by a secret revolutionary group which was dissatisfied with the government.

The Revolution of 1905 forced the Tsar to make some reforms, but they were not great enough.

factories, schools, banks, and telegraph offices closed down. Peasants also attacked the estates of wealthy landowners. Tsar Nicholas II was frightened by this revolt. To please the people, he permitted them to elect an assembly called the Duma to help make the nation's laws. The Duma had little power, however.

The Russian people overthrow their government. On March 12, 1917, huge crowds of angry people swarmed through the streets of Russia's capital city. They were angry for good reasons. About two and a half years earlier, World War I* had started, and Russian soldiers had marched off to fight against the Germans. However, the Russian government was so careless that the army was not being given enough food, clothing, and ammunition. Here in the city, many people were hungry, too. The crowds grew larger, and the officers ordered soldiers to scatter them. Instead of obeying, the troops joined the angry crowds.

Since the Tsar's government could no longer keep order, members of the Duma quickly chose a committee of men to govern the country. On March 20, they placed the Tsar under arrest. The new leaders tried to establish a democratic form of government in Russia. They faced many problems, however. Russia was still fighting in World War I. Many people were restless and dissatisfied. It would take time to bring order and happiness to the nation.

DO YOU KNOW

1. Using the map on page 34, tell how the Slavs united to form Kievan Russia.
2. With the help of the picture on page 36, tell what happened to Kievan Russia. How were the Russians reunited?
3. How did Russia gain its great empire?
4. Why were many Russians dissatisfied?
5. What important events took place in 1917?

Nicholas II was forced to leave his throne in 1917. The new leaders wanted Russia to be a democracy.

Marx was a German thinker who gave the Communists many of their ideas about government.

CHAPTER FOUR
MODERN HISTORY

One April evening in 1917, a month after the Tsar* of Russia was overthrown, a great crowd of people gathered at a railroad station in Petrograd,* the capital city of Russia. They had come to welcome home a short, almost bald man called V. I. Lenin.

Lenin was a leader of the Communists, who gained control of Russia. The Communist government took over all the land and industries.

Lenin was one of the leaders of the Bolshevik Party, a group that had secretly plotted to overthrow the Tsar's government. He had spent the last ten years in western Europe, for it had not been safe for him to live in Russia while the Tsar ruled. Now, however, the Tsar had been arrested and Lenin was coming home.

Lenin and the other members of the Bolshevik Party were not satisfied with the democratic type of government which had been established after the Tsar was forced to leave his throne. They planned to overthrow this government and make many changes in Russia.

A nineteenth-century German thinker named Karl Marx had given the Bolsheviks many of their ideas. At the time he lived, people who owned factories and mines were very wealthy. Workers in these industries were wretchedly poor, however, for they received very low wages.

Marx did not know that as time went on workers in privately owned industries would earn more money and live well. He thought the only way they could hope to have a better life was to gain control of the government and take away the rich people's property. Then, when the working people were in power, they would not allow private individuals to own farms, factories, or mines. Everything would belong to all the workers together and be run by the government. Some of Marx's followers thought this change should be brought about slowly and peacefully. However, Lenin and the other Bolsheviks thought that workers throughout the world should take over as quickly as possible, even by fighting if necessary. These people who believed in world revolution came to be known as "Communists."

Under Lenin's leadership, the Communists grew very powerful in Russia. They promised to give the people peace, bread, and

Women soldiers in Petrograd.* Women as well as men fought in the Communist Revolution of 1917.

land. Because these promises sounded good, many hungry, war-weary Russians began to support the Communists.

The Communists seize power. On November 7, 1917, the Communists attacked the Winter Palace, where the government headquarters were located. The officials there were arrested, and a new government was quickly set up. A peace treaty was signed with Germany, and the nation's capital was moved to the city of Moscow. Soon all the land, forests, mines, and factories in the country were taken over by the government, just as the Communists had planned.

The new leaders did not permit anyone to disagree with them publicly. They did not allow free elections where the people could vote to change their country's leadership if they didn't like it. To make sure they stayed in power, the Communists established a

Formerly wealthy people sold their belongings after the Communists gained control.

special police force called the Cheka to arrest and execute anyone suspected of opposing the government.

The country is torn by civil war. Bitter fighting broke out in Russia after the Communists seized power. Many Russians did not agree with the new rulers and tried to overthrow them. Foreign countries which did not feel that the Communists were the rightful leaders of Russia sent troops into the country. Conquered nations in the Russian Empire also fought to win back their independence.

The Communists organized a large army to fight all these enemies. For more than two years, the country was torn by warfare. By 1921, most of the Communists' enemies had been defeated, but Russia lay in ruins. Millions of people were starving, and factories had almost stopped producing goods.

The government encourages the people to rebuild their country. The Communists knew that they had to make life better for the people or they would be overthrown. To encourage the peasants* to produce more food, they permitted them to run their farms as though

The Communists handed out newspapers that urged people to support the new government.

they owned them. They also allowed people to own and operate small factories. Within seven years the Russian people had nearly rebuilt their country.

The new leaders made another important change. They changed the country's name from Russia to the Union of Soviet Socialist Republics, which we often call the Soviet Union.

Stalin becomes the dictator* of the Soviet Union. When Lenin died, in 1924, several different rivals tried to take his place. Among them was a stocky, dark-haired man called Joseph Stalin. Stalin was clever and cruel. As he became more and more powerful, he had his enemies executed or exiled. Finally, no one in the country dared to criticize or disobey him. Now the people had fewer rights and freedoms than they had under the tsars.

The Five-Year Plans are started. Stalin wanted to make the Soviet Union a great industrial nation. He believed this could be done most quickly and successfully if the government planned and directed all the work in the country.

In 1928 the government announced the goals it wanted the nation to reach within the next five years. All the private factories would be taken over by the government. New industries would be started, and new electric power plants built. These would be built only by the government. Large, government-controlled farms would also be established to provide the industrial workers with food. (See page 84.) Because all these goals were to be achieved in five years, this was called the Five-Year Plan.

The Soviet government had other Five-Year Plans after the first one. Many new mills and factories were built, but the people suffered great hardships. Workers received little pay for their work. The government often took so much of the peasants' crops that they had little for themselves.

Children in an orphanage after World War II. The war brought great suffering to the Soviet Union.

The Soviet people fight the Germans in World War II.* In 1941, German troops suddenly invaded the Soviet Union. Cities were bombed and shelled, and millions of Soviet people lost their lives. The United States and other countries who were also fighting Germany sent tanks, ammunition, and other supplies to help the Soviet army. During the war, the Soviet Union and these nations were allies.*

Soviet tanks in Hungary. Communist governments have been established by force in many countries.

Other nations become suspicious of the Soviet Union. After the war ended, the Soviet Union did several things which made other nations suspicious of her. Communist governments were set up by force in many neighboring nations which the Soviet army had occupied during the war. These governments were forced to take orders from the Soviet leaders. The Soviet Union also wanted Communist governments to be established in China, Korea, and other countries. It was clear that the Soviet leaders hoped to bring the rest of the world under communism. The United States and other nations that did not believe in communism agreed to work together to protect themselves against this threat.

The Soviet Union today. Stalin's harsh rule of the Soviet Union ended when he died, in 1953. The Soviet leaders who followed him have tried to make other nations less suspicious of the Soviet Union. Nikita S. Khrushchev, one of the most important of these men, has traveled to many countries and made many speeches in favor of peace. However, like Lenin, he and the other Communist leaders still believe that Communist governments should be established in all other countries. They are working to bring this about.

DO YOU KNOW

1. Use the pictures and text in this chapter to tell who the Communists are and where they got their ideas. Who was Lenin?
2. Tell how the Communists gained control of Russia. What happened afterward?
3. What are the Five-Year Plans?
4. Why did other nations become suspicious of the Soviet Union after World War II?

The growth of Soviet electric power is shown on this map. Soviet power plants are government owned.

Celebrating the Communist Revolution. The Soviet government is controlled by the Communist Party.

CHAPTER FIVE
GOVERNMENT

The people of the Soviet Union are not permitted to help decide how their country should be run. They must follow the orders of a small group of men whom they did not elect to be their rulers. These men are the leaders of the only political party in the Soviet Union — the Communist Party.

Who belongs to the Communist Party? We would expect most of the Soviet people to belong to the party that runs their country. This is not true, however. Less than four out of every hundred people in the Soviet Union are Party members. High government officials and most of the factory managers and other people who hold important positions are members of the Party.

The Communist Party chooses its members very carefully. Only a person who shows that he agrees wholeheartedly with what the Party does is allowed to join. He must be a hard worker and do exactly what the Party leaders order or he might lose his membership. He doesn't want this to happen for several reasons. As long as he belongs to the Party, he is more important than his friends and neighbors. He can have a better job, a bigger apartment, and longer vacations than most people.

Soviet officials meet with foreign visitors. All important government officials are Communists.

How is the Communist Party organized? The Communist Party is organized very much like an army. In an army the general and his staff decide what should be done. They pass their orders down to officers who tell the soldiers what to do. In the Communist Party, Nikita Khrushchev decides how the Party should be run. He is the chairman of a group of about fifteen men called the Party Presidium. These men help him make his decisions. Orders from the Presidium are sent to Communist officials. They pass the orders down to the Party members, who attend meetings once a month in factories, offices, and farms where they work. One of the most important jobs these ordinary members have is to

Khrushchev talks to Nixon. Khrushchev heads the group of men who run the Party and the government.

convince their friends and fellow workers that everything the Communist leaders do is right. They are also supposed to find out what the people are thinking and let their leaders know.

How did Khrushchev and the other leaders gain their power? The ordinary people who belong to the Communist Party do not choose the men who run their Party. Their leaders gained power by cleverly and ruthlessly getting rid of their enemies. They will keep their power until someone stronger takes it away.

The Rules* of the Communist Party, however, make it appear as though ordinary members really do choose their leaders and help run the Party. According to the rules, Communists from all over the country are supposed to come together at least every four years for a meeting called the All-Union Communist Party Congress. This congress elects about 130 of its members to form a Central Committee, and the Central Committee elects the men of the Party Presidium.

These elections are not like elections in democratic organizations, however. The people at the All-Union Communist Congress may not decide for themselves what people to vote for. The candidates were chosen beforehand by Khrushchev and the other members of the Presidium. There is only one name listed for each office. These people were chosen because they could be depended upon to support the leaders.

The Communists control the Soviet government. The fifteen men who run the Communist Party also control the Soviet government. If we were in a Soviet city on election day, we would see one important way they do this. When we looked at a ballot, we would notice that only one name was listed for each government office. This person was selected by the Communists because he was a member of the Party or was someone outside the Party who was loyal to the Communists. Everyone eighteen years of age or older is expected to vote for him. In this way, the Communists make sure that all government offices in the Soviet Union are held by people who will follow orders from the Party leaders.

The main reason the Communists bother holding elections is to make the people feel as though they are taking part in their government. This helps to keep people from becoming dissatisfied. As we learn more about the Soviet government, we will see how cleverly it was planned to look democratic. We will also see that it is really not democratic at all. The Communist leaders do just as they please.

The Soviet Union has a constitution. The Soviet Union has a constitution that explains how the government is supposed to be run. When we read this constitution, it sounds very democratic. It

Voting in the Soviet Union is a simple process. There is only one candidate for each office.

The Soviet Union is made up of fifteen republics. Several of these were once independent countries.

promises the people freedom to say what they want, to hold meetings, and to print whatever they please in newspapers and books. The Communists, however, prevent the people from enjoying these freedoms. No one is allowed to print or say anything of which the government does not approve.

The Soviet Union is a union of fifteen republics. The constitution says that the Soviet Union is a union of fifteen republics which have joined together willingly to form one nation. Page 80 will help to show that they did not all become a part of the

Soviet Union as willingly as the constitution might lead us to believe. The largest and most powerful republic in the country is the Russian Soviet Federated Socialist Republic. (See map on page 61.)

The constitution states that any of the fifteen republics have the right to become independent countries whenever they want to. This could never happen as long as the Communists remain in power, however. The governing officials in all the republics were carefully checked by the Communist Party before they could be elected. They can be depended upon to obey orders given by the Party leaders in Moscow.

The Supreme Soviet is supposed to make the country's laws. The constitution also states that the country's laws are to be made by an assembly called the Supreme Soviet. The men and women who are elected to be members of this assembly meet in Moscow, the capital city, for one week twice each year. In that short time, they could not possibly make the laws the nation needs. All they really do is vote "yes" for laws that were prepared beforehand by the Communist leaders.

When we read the Soviet constitution, this may not seem to be true. The constitution says that the Supreme Soviet is to elect a committee called the Presidium of the Supreme Soviet. This committee prepares the laws when the Supreme Soviet is not in session. Don't forget, however, that the Communists decide in advance who shall be elected to the Presidium of the Supreme Soviet. Some of these people are important Communists who also belong to the Party Presidium. They make the laws that Khrushchev and his top officials want.

The laws are carried out by the Council of Ministers. According to the constitution, the Supreme Soviet is supposed to choose a group of men called the Council of Ministers to carry out the country's laws. Really, however, the leaders of the Communist Party choose the men they want, and the Supreme Soviet just approves them. Many of the men on the Council of Ministers are important Communists. Some also belong to the Party Presidium. The men on the Council of Ministers are put in charge of different departments, or ministries, of the government.

The laws are enforced by the courts. The Soviet Union has courts which decide if people accused of breaking the law are guilty and how they should be punished. Crimes like stealing and breaking

The Supreme Soviet in session. This lawmaking assembly meets for one week twice each year.

traffic laws are tried in people's courts. There are no juries in these courts. Instead, two ordinary citizens help the judge decide if a person is guilty or not. The judges in people's courts do not need to have any training in law. If a person does not think he had a fair trial in one of the people's courts, he may take his case to a higher court. The highest court in the country is the Supreme Court of the U.S.S.R. in Moscow.

In the Soviet Union, people who are accused of crimes like breaking traffic rules usually get fair trials, but people accused of working against the government often do not. The Communists believe that the courts should be used to protect their Party's power. They expect Soviet judges and lawyers to agree with them if they say a person is guilty.

Visitors at a people's court. Two citizens help the judge decide if a person is guilty.

A village council meeting. Local affairs are run by councils, called soviets.

The governments of republics, counties, and cities. Each of the fifteen republics has its own supreme soviet, presidium, and council of ministers. The people in the counties and in the cities elect councils, called soviets, to run their affairs. Of course, the people they elect were approved by the Communist Party. These people do just as the Communist leaders say.

How does the Communist Party keep its power? When we remember that less than four out of every hundred Soviet citizens are members of the Communist Party, we wonder how the Communists are able to control the country so completely. One reason is that

Tanks on parade. The powerful Soviet army is controlled by the Communist Party.

most Soviet people are afraid of them. The Communist Party has many spies. Because the people are not sure who may be a spy, they are afraid to speak their feelings about the Communist leaders to anyone. They don't want to be accused of working against the government because it is hard for them to prove they are innocent. Once the courts decide they are guilty, they may be sent to forced labor camps or prisons, or be executed. The powerful Soviet army is also controlled by the Communists. It would be used quickly to stop any revolts.

In addition to frightening the people into obedience, the Communists work hard to convince them that they are happy under the kind of government they have. In their youth clubs and schools, children are taught to believe that the Communist leaders are wise, and that their kind of government is good. Books, movies, newspaper articles, and television and radio programs that criticize communism or give a fair picture of life in other countries are not allowed. For this reason, the people do not have a chance to compare honestly the way they live with life in democratic countries. When the Communist leaders tell them that their system of government is the best kind, many people in the Soviet Union really believe this is true.

DO YOU KNOW

1. Explain how the Communist Party of the Soviet Union is organized. How does it control the Soviet government?
2. How many people are Party members?
3. Why do the Communists hold elections?
4. What is the Supreme Soviet? Name one important way in which it differs from the United States Congress.

Making a movie. In the Soviet Union, no one may make a movie that criticizes communism.

Factory workers in Moscow. About half the people of the Soviet Union are Russians.

CHAPTER SIX
THE PEOPLE

Many different groups of people live in the Soviet Union. Can you imagine combining all the countries of Europe to form one giant country? The Soviet Union is a combination of nations much like this. People of about 175 different nationalities live within its borders. They do not speak the same language, and many of them dress and live in different ways. The Early History Chapter, which begins on page 34, helps to explain how they became part of the same country.

The Russians. The largest group of people in the Soviet Union are the Russians. They make up about half of the country's population. Their ancestors were people called Slavs. They were living in the western part of the country at the time that Christ was born. The map below shows where the Russians live today.

Most of the Russian people we see as we walk through the streets of Moscow are rather short and stocky, and many of them have fair hair. They are dressed much as we are, but their clothes are not so well made as ours. The Soviet leaders want their country's factories to produce mining machinery, factory equipment, and rockets, rather than nice clothing for the people.

Main groups of people in the Soviet Union. About three fourths of the people are of Slavic descent.

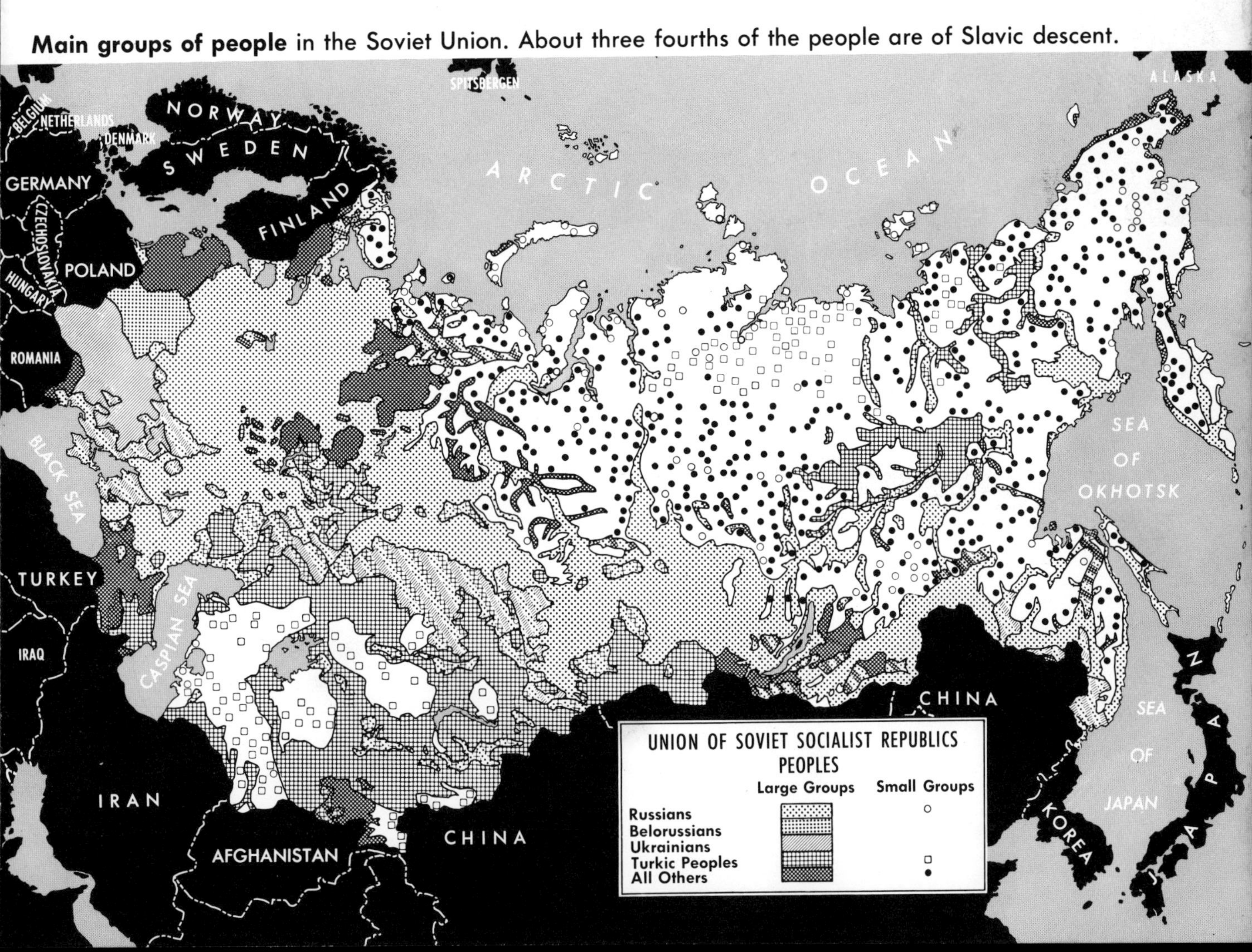

Now we stop at an outdoor newsstand to buy a magazine. When we hand the man our money, he says, "Spasebo," which means "thank you" in Russian. This is the official language of the Soviet Union. The words in the Russian magazine we bought are written in an alphabet different from ours. It is called the Cyrillic* alphabet. Some of the letters look the same as ours, but they do not sound the same. For example, the letter "P" is pronounced the way we say "R."

A world map printed in Russian. This is the official language of the Soviet Union.

A church service in Moscow. Church members may not belong to the Communist Party.

At one corner, we pass a large church that is now used as a museum. For a long time, a branch of the Christian religion called Russian Orthodox* was the official religion of the Russians. After the Communists came to power, however, most of the churches were closed. The Communists told the people that there was no God and tried to prevent them from worshiping. Today some churches are still open, and people in the Soviet Union are permitted to worship if they want to. However, church members may not belong to the Communist Party, and children are taught in school that there is no God.

Many of the people we pass live in apartments. Whole families are often crowded into one or two small rooms. They usually share a kitchen and bathroom with other families in the building. Though new apartment buildings are being constructed, it will be a long time before there are enough for most people to have comfortable places in which to live. The best apartments now are saved for government officials, scientists, factory managers, and other important people.

When we get to know some Russian people, we find that we like them very much. Most of them are kind and helpful. They enjoy sports, movies, and music, just as we do. They have strong emotions, and when they love someone or are unhappy they are not ashamed to show it.

A Russian family in Moscow. Russian people enjoy many of the same things we do.

Ukrainians building a wall. About one sixth of the people in the Soviet Union are Ukrainians.

The Ukrainians. Now let us travel to the wide grasslands that lie southwest of Moscow and visit a group of people called the Ukrainians. They make up about one sixth of the country's population. Like the Russians, they are descended from the Slavs. They also dress and live very much like their Russian neighbors. However, they speak their own language and think of themselves as a separate nationality from the Russians.

Most of the Ukrainians we see are tall, and many have dark hair. They seem to be a gay, light-hearted people. On holidays and special occasions, they dress in the colorful costumes of earlier days and do lively folk dances.

Belorussians usually have fair skin and blond hair. They live in the western part of the country.

The Belorussians. In the wooded lands that lie west of Moscow, we may visit a group of people called the Belorussians. Less than one twentieth of the country's people belong to this group. The Belorussians are also descended from the Slavs. Most of them are poorer than the Russians and Ukrainians, however, for the region in which they live does not have good soil or rich mineral deposits. Belorussians are usually blond and have fair skin. Perhaps this is how they got their name, for "belo" is the Slavic* word for "white."

The Georgians and Armenians. In the rugged Caucasus region live two groups of dark-haired people called the Georgians and the Armenians. (See map on page 61.) Their ancestors have lived in this part of the country for thousands of years. They were writing fine poetry and building beautiful cities long before Columbus discovered America. At one time Georgia and Armenia were both independent kingdoms. They were among the first nations in the world to accept Christianity.

Today, there are nearly three million Armenians and more than two and a half million Georgians in the Soviet Union. Some of the Soviet Union's best-known people have come from these two nationalities. Joseph Stalin was a Georgian. Several fine scientists and artists come from Armenia.

Armenians playing folk music. There are nearly three million Armenians in the Soviet Union.

The descendants of tribesmen from Asia. Nearly one tenth of the Soviet people are descended from dark-haired Turkic tribesmen who were living in the desert region more than a thousand years ago. The map on page 69 shows where these people live. Some of these people have brownish skin, and eyes that appear to be slanted. Their Turkic ancestors married warlike invaders called Mongols, who swept into the country from the lands lying north of China.

The descendants of the Turkic people and the Mongols are divided into many different groups. Most of them earn their living as shepherds or farmers. We have time to visit only the largest

An Uzbek store. Many people of the desert region are descendants of Turkic tribesmen.

An Uzbek family. People in the desert region live much as people do in neighboring Asian countries.

group, the Uzbeks, who live near the southern border of the Soviet Union. (See map on page 61.)

On our way to the Uzbek city of Samarkand, we pass through mile after mile of desert wasteland. As we approach the mountains that border the desert on the south, we see villages of mud-brick houses surrounded by orchards and green fields. Mountain streams bring water to these oases.* Some of the Uzbek men working in the fields are wearing striped, knee-length robes tied at the waist with bright sashes. This is their national costume.

Ahead of us lies Samarkand. Above the roofs of the houses rise the blue domes of several mosques. These are the religious buildings of the Islamic* faith. Like most people descended from the Turkic tribesmen, the Uzbeks have followed this religion for centuries. The Communists have closed many mosques, however, and are trying to make the people believe that all religions are false.

We are driving into the city now. Ahead of us is a man leading a donkey loaded with fresh peaches and apricots. An older woman wearing a veil over her face is turning the corner. This city and its people remind us that this part of the Soviet Union lies in Asia.

Primitive tribesmen. Far north of the desert, in the forests of Siberia and along the lonely Arctic coast are many small tribes of

Praying in a mosque. Many people in the Caucasus and the desert region follow the Islamic faith.

A Siberian tribesman. Many of the primitive tribesmen in Siberia are hunters and fishermen.

people who still live in a primitive manner. Some of them live in rude shelters made of poles and animal skins. Part of these people make their living by herding reindeer, and part are hunters and fishermen. These tribes are often different from one another in appearance. Some look like Eskimos. Others remind us of the American Indians.

Other groups of people. We can mention only a few of the other groups of people who live in the Soviet Union. Descendants of people from the neighboring country of Iran live in several places

Estonians in national costume. Before 1940, Estonia, Latvia, and Lithuania were independent.

along the southern border. There are also groups of Jews in the country. In 1940, the small nations of Latvia, Lithuania, and Estonia were taken over by the Soviet Union, and their people are now Soviet citizens.

Bitter hardships have been suffered by many of the smaller groups of people who were forced to become a part of the Soviet

Union. The Russians, who form the largest group in the country, hold most of the nation's power. Nearly all of the important Communist leaders are Russians. They encourage the Russian people to feel proud of their past. It is dangerous, however, for the smaller groups of people to show too much pride in the deeds of their ancestors. The Communists say that they are not being loyal to the Soviet Union when they do so.

Some nationalities in the Soviet Union have been completely uprooted because they were said to be disloyal. They have been forced to leave their homes. Some were sent to work as slaves in forced labor camps in remote parts of the country.

The Soviet Union is not a crowded country. Altogether, there are more than 208 million people in the Soviet Union. This is about thirty million more than live in the United States. However, when

The Soviet Union is not crowded, although more than 208 million people live there.

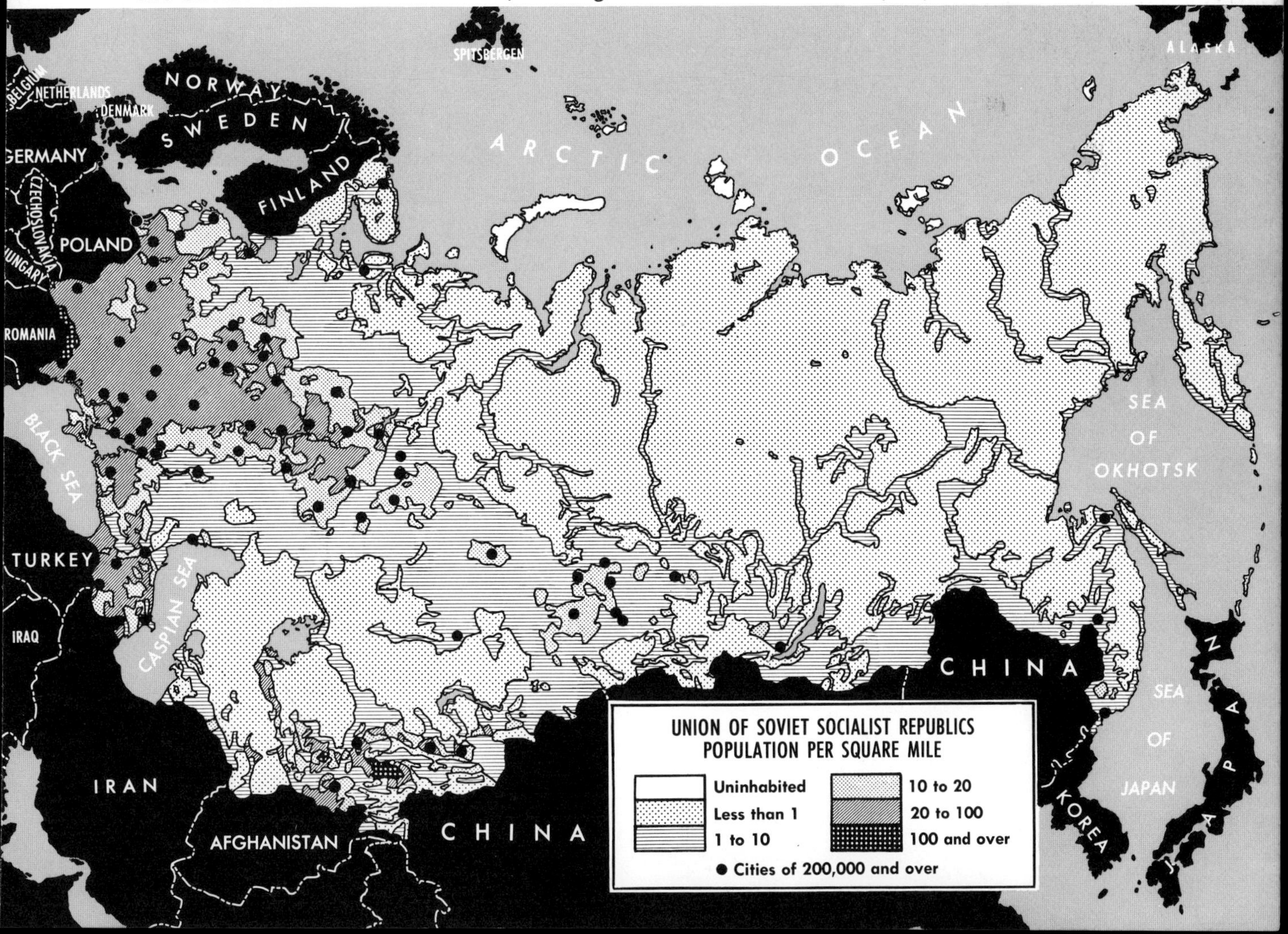

we remember that the Soviet Union is about two and a half times the size of the United States, we can see that it is not at all crowded.

The Soviet people are moving eastward. The map on page 81 shows that most of the people in the Soviet Union live in the western part of the country. In recent years, however, new government farms, mines, and factories have been established in the eastern part. The government is strongly encouraging many people from the crowded cities of the west to take new jobs in the east.

DO YOU KNOW

1. How many different groups of people live in the Soviet Union? Which is the largest?
2. What is the official language of the Soviet Union? What alphabet does it use?
3. Describe the kind of apartments in which many Moscow people live.
4. Why are many Soviet people moving eastward?

New housing in Vladivostok. Many people are taking new jobs in the eastern part of the country.

On a Soviet farm. Almost half the working people in the Soviet Union earn their living on farms.

CHAPTER SEVEN

FARMING AND GRAZING

Almost one half of the working people in the Soviet Union earn their living by farming. This is about ten times as many farm workers as there are in the United States. Yet the Soviet Union does not produce as much food as the United States does each year. Let us find out why.

Soviet farm workers do not own their farms. Not a single person in the Soviet Union owns his farm. After the Communists gained control of the country in 1917, all the nation's farmland was taken over by the government. It was then divided into small farms. For about ten years the peasants* were allowed to work on these farms just as though they owned them. Then in 1928, a great change was made.

"We need more food for our workers in the cities," said the government leaders. "Our peasants must stop using wooden plows and old-fashioned farming methods. They must begin to use tractors and other large machines. This can't be done well on the small plots of land they have now. We will have to group their little farms together to form large ones called collective farms."

"We don't want to give up our farms and work on collective farms," said the peasants. Many of them tried to resist, but they were killed or forced to work as slaves in lumber camps in distant Siberia.

In the end the Communists had their way. Most Soviet peasants today work on collective farms. These farms must sell a large part of their products to the government at any price the government wishes to pay. Part of the money the farm earns is used to pay taxes and to buy tractors and other necessary things. The money that is left over after the farm has paid its expenses is divided among the workers according to the kind of work each has done.

In addition to collective farms, the Soviet Union has large state farms. They turn over all of their products to the government. Workers on state farms earn regular wages like factory workers.

The Soviet government is doing several things to encourage farmers to produce more food. Until recently, collective farms received very little for the products which the government bought.

Khrushchev congratulates successful collective farmers. Soviet people do not own their farms.

Because the farm workers knew they would not get much for their work, they became discouraged and produced little. The Soviet government is now paying more for the farm products it buys. It also gives medals and other awards to people who produce more than their fellow workers. Even so, Soviet farm workers do not raise as much food as farmers in the United States do.

Soviet farms do not have enough fertilizer and farm machinery. One important reason Soviet farm workers do not produce more food is that they don't have all the fertilizer and farm machinery they

A new tractor on display. Soviet farmers need more farm machinery and fertilizer.

need. Sometimes, too, there are not enough parts to repair machines that have broken down. The Soviet leaders believe it is more important to build factory machines, rockets, and military equipment than tractors and combines.*

Only one tenth of the Soviet Union is suitable for growing crops. Another reason the Soviet Union does not produce more food is that much of the country is not good for farming. In many places, there is too little rainfall. (See map on page 28.) Huge swamps, rugged mountains, and poor soils make much of the land unfit for farming. Also, the Soviet Union lies so close to the North Pole that summers are too short and cool in the northern part of the country for many crops to ripen.

Even so, the Soviet Union has more farmland than the United States. Most of it is in a large triangle of land that stretches from the western border to about the center of the country. This is called the Fertile Triangle. (See map below.) Summers in this region are long enough for crops to ripen. The rainfall map on page 28 shows another reason why farming is important here. In the southern part of the Fertile Triangle the soil is very rich and black. This is sometimes called the Black Earth Country.

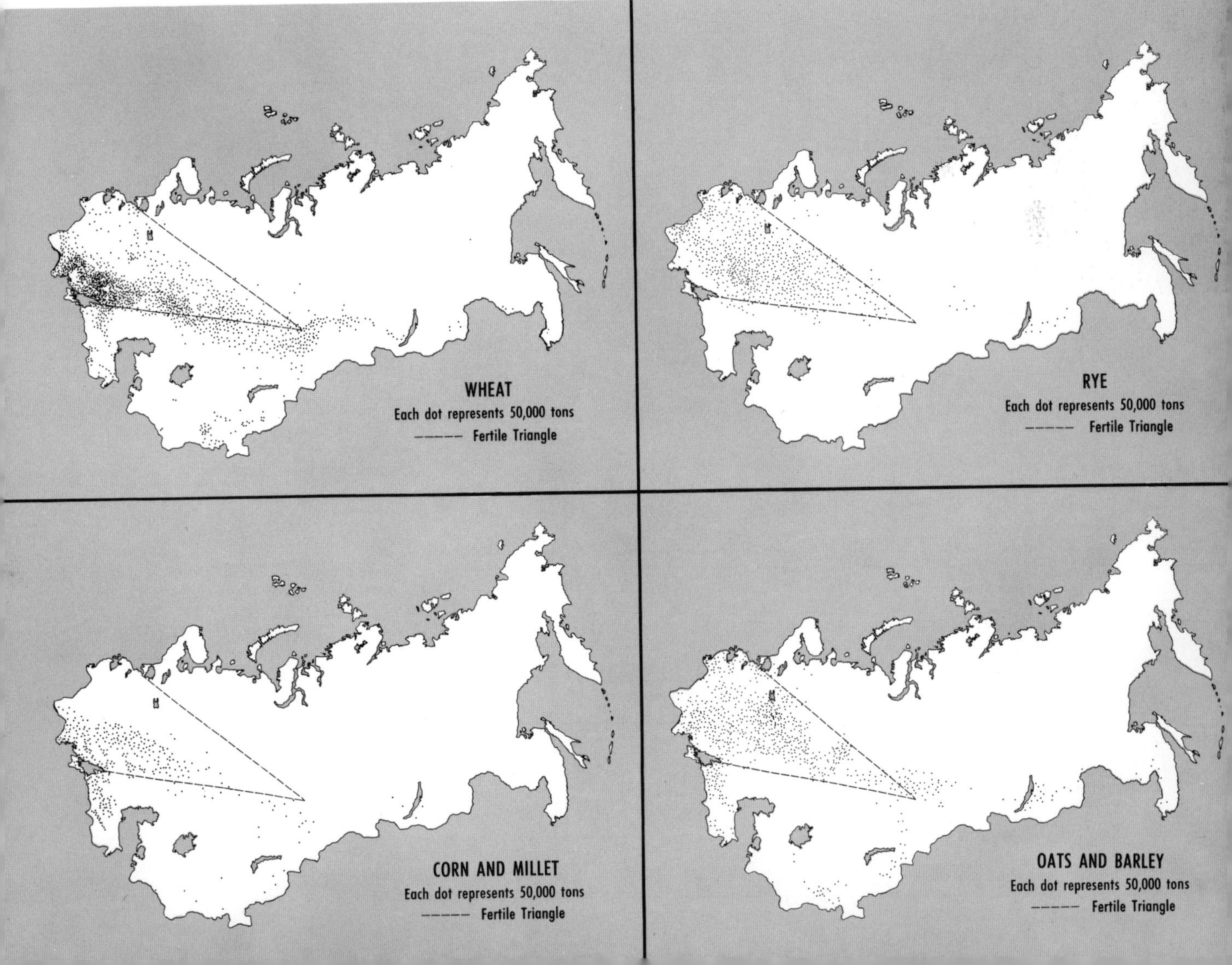

Grain is the Soviet Union's main crop. Most of the country's farmland is in the Fertile Triangle.

Grain is the Soviet Union's main crop. Imagine that we are walking through a field of rustling wheat in the Black Earth Country. In the distance, some men are operating a giant combine. Beyond them, more fields of golden grain stretch on as far as we can see.

A farm worker nearby tells us that more farmland in the Soviet Union is planted in grain than in any other crop. He explains that rye, barley, and oats are the most important grains in the northern part of the Fertile Triangle, where the climate is cool and the soil is not very rich. Here in the southern part, the hot summers and black soil are good for growing wheat. In fact, so much wheat is grown here that this is called the breadbasket of the country. This region, however, does not always have enough rainfall for crops to grow well.

Wheat grows well in the region of black soils in the southern part of the Fertile Triangle.

Flax is raised in the northern part of the Fertile Triangle, where the climate is cool.

The Soviet Union needs more grain than it now produces. The government has started new farms along the northern edge of the desert and in Siberia to provide this grain. However, the climate in these areas is sometimes too cold or dry for farming.

Soviet farms need to raise more livestock. Now we leave the wheat field and walk to the barns and pens where cattle, hogs, and other livestock are kept. Here we meet a young man who tells us that he is the farm veterinarian, or animal doctor.

The young man says that this farm, like most other Soviet farms, does not raise as much livestock as it would like to. There are not enough good barns to shelter the livestock during the long, cold winter. There is not enough feed either, for most of the grain raised here is needed to make bread and cereal for people to eat. He tells

A shepherd in the Caucasus. Many sheep graze on mountain slopes and at the edge of the desert.

us that the government is encouraging the peasants to build more barns and to raise more corn for feed.

Even though the Soviet Union is not now able to raise as many hogs and cattle as it would like, it does have many sheep. They can live in places that are too dry to raise grain or to graze cattle. Many are raised on steep mountain slopes in the Caucasus region and at the edge of the desert. (Compare map on page 13 with the map below.) Others are raised here in the Fertile Triangle.

Potatoes and other crops grow in the Fertile Triangle. We ask the young man what else besides livestock and grain is raised in the Fertile Triangle. He says that potatoes and sugar beets are two very important crops. (See map on page 92.) Fresh vegetables are

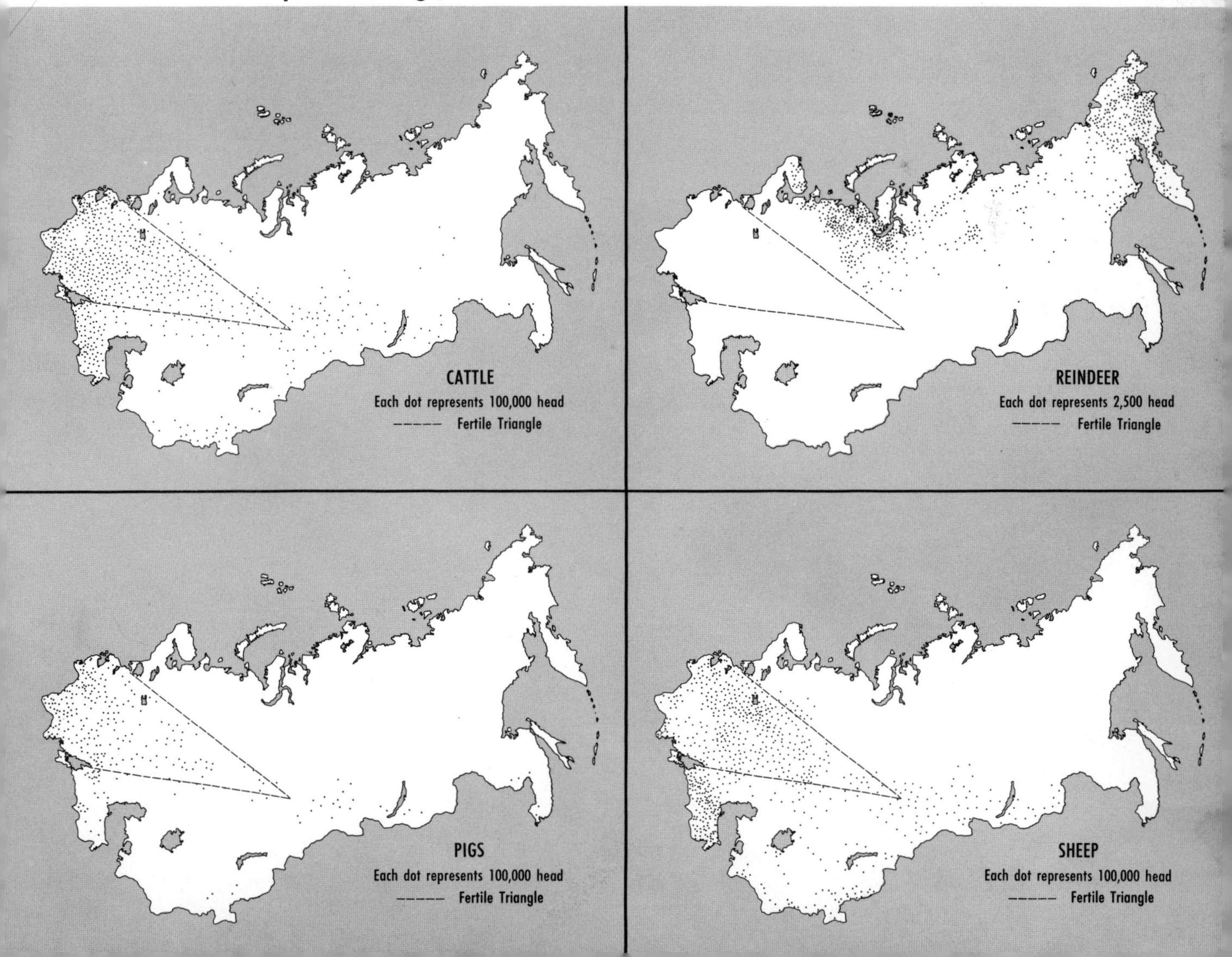

Sheep, cattle, hogs, and reindeer are raised in the Soviet Union.

raised on farms near the cities. Here in the south, golden sunflowers also grow in many places. Their seeds provide oil for cooking and for making soap. Farther north, where the climate is cooler, there are many fields of flax. The fibers obtained from this plant are used to make linen cloth. Its seeds, called linseed, supply oil.

Warm-weather crops grow near the Black Sea. We leave the farm now and travel southward to the farmlands that lie near the Black Sea in the Caucasus region. (See map on page 13.) Here, in addition to sheep and grain, we see warm-weather crops such as tea, lemons, and grapes. These crops grow well because the high Caucasus Mountains shelter this region from cold winter winds. There is plenty of rainfall, too.

Important crops of the Soviet Union are potatoes, sugar beets, sunflowers, cotton, and linseed.

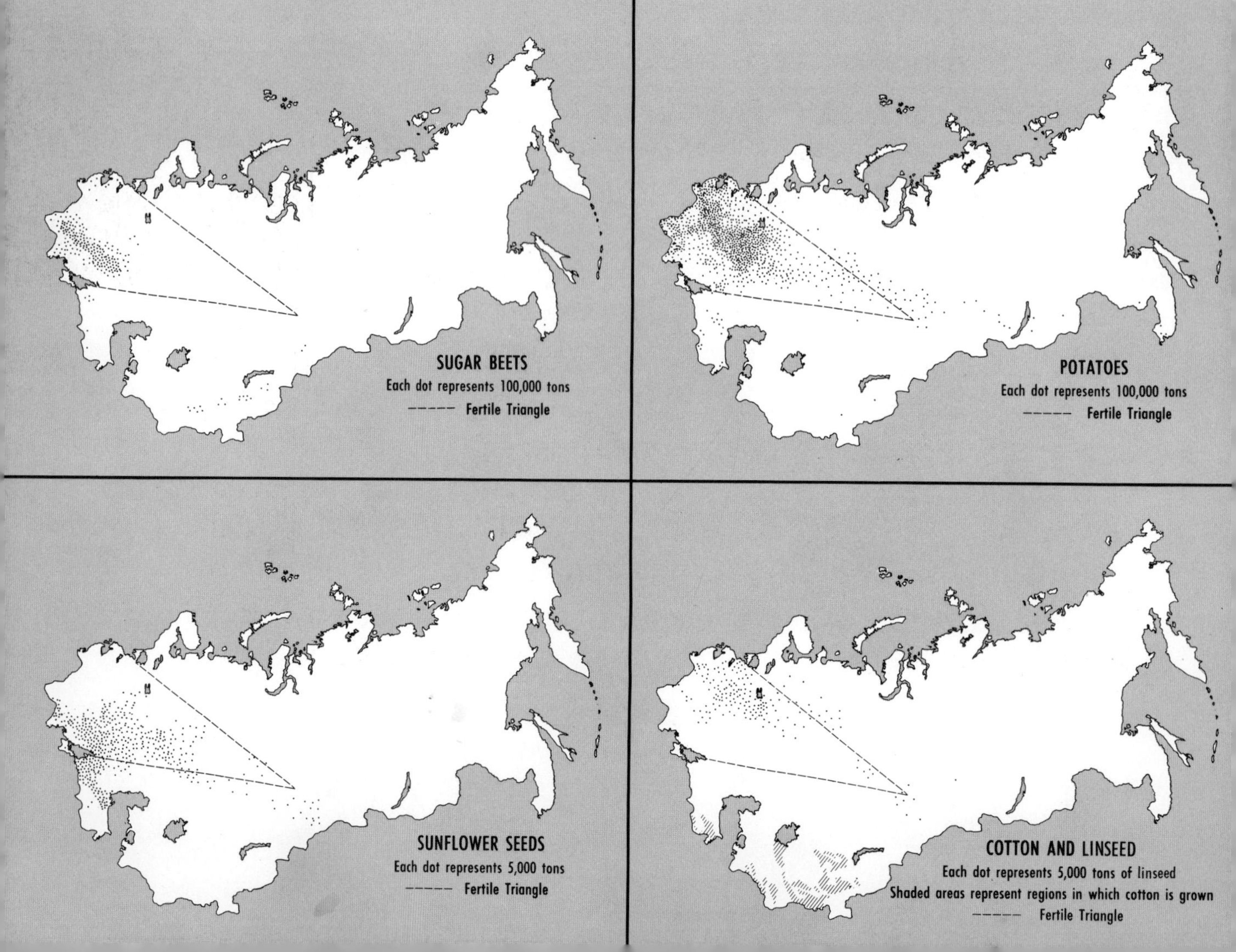

Picking tea leaves. Tea and other warm-weather crops are grown near the Black Sea.

Cotton and other crops grow near the border of the desert. Now we visit the farmlands at the foot of the mountains that lie along the southern border of the desert region. (See map on page 13.) Many of the farm workers we meet here raise cotton, for the summers this far south are very hot. So little rain falls in this region that long ditches have been dug to bring water from mountain rivers to the thirsty fields. Other crops besides cotton grow in these irrigated lands. We see many fields of grain and orchards of fruit trees here.

Farming in other parts of the country. There are other farmlands in the Soviet Union in addition to the ones we visited. They are scattered through the forests and near the Pacific coast. The peasants in many of these places are very poor, for the summers are short and the soils too poor for crops to grow well.

DO YOU KNOW

1. Tell how collective farms were established in the Soviet Union. How are workers on these farms paid?
2. Give two reasons why the Soviet Union does not produce more food.
3. Where is most of the Soviet Union's good farmland? Why do crops grow well here?
4. What is the Soviet Union's main crop?

Digging potatoes in Siberia. Much of this region has poor soil and a short growing season.

A farm village in the Soviet Union. Soviet farm workers usually live in villages.

CHAPTER EIGHT

A VISIT TO A COLLECTIVE FARM VILLAGE

It is a warm, sunny day in August, and we are on our way to visit a farm village in the grassland region of the Soviet Union. Our automobile leaves a cloud of dust behind us as we drive over the rutted dirt road. On either side of the road are fields of ripening grain. Ahead of us we see the blue, onion-shaped dome of an old church. Near the church are groups of small white houses. The people who live here work together on one big farm called a collective farm.

Making plans for spring planting. Each collective farm has a chairman and a managing committee.

Soon we enter the village and stop in front of the church. An old woman carrying a pail of water from the village well tells us that services have not been held here since the government closed the churches many years ago. While we are talking to her, a man comes out of the square, whitewashed building across the street. When he introduces himself, we learn that he is Mr. Nikolaev, the chairman of this farm.

Mr. Nikolaev tells us that the building across the street is the headquarters of the village. He invites us inside. One room is his office. In another room we see several women adding long columns of numbers in thick books. They are figuring out how much money the farm has earned. Mr. Nikolaev explains that the money the farm has left over after it has paid its taxes and other expenses is divided among the farm workers. They are paid according to the kind of work each has done.

Now Mr. Nikolaev offers to show us the rest of the village. First we walk next door to the village nursery, where babies and small children stay while their mothers work in the fields. The babies look as though they were snuggled inside cocoons, for they are tightly wrapped in long strips of cloth from the waist down. Across the street from the nursery we see a little hospital. The villagers receive free medical care here. A short way down the road is the

Children in farm villages learn how to operate tractors and other farm machinery.

school. Nearby is a new building. Mr. Nikolaev tells us that this is the community hall. The villagers come here for meetings, movies, and dancing.

Farther down the road, across a narrow field, we see some farm buildings. Several of them are barns where the village cows and horses are kept. There is also a pigsty and a square silo dug into the ground where cattle feed is stored.

We decide to drive our car on the rest of the tour, for the farm is very large. Altogether, it covers nearly fifteen thousand acres. The workers have to walk or ride in horse-drawn carts to the fields each day, for there are only six trucks and one car in the whole village.

A community hall. The villagers come to the hall for meetings, movies, and dancing.

Farm workers are grouped into brigades. Many of the workers are women.

The people we see on the farm are working in groups, called brigades. Mr. Nikolaev explains that each of these brigades has a special job to do. One takes care of the pigs, another works in the grainfields, and so on.

We stop to watch a brigade harvesting a large field of grain. More than half of the workers are women. They are wearing skirts and blouses and have white kerchiefs on their heads. It seems to us that there are more workers than necessary in the field.

On our way back to the village, we pass a boy who is driving a flock of geese. We decide to get out and visit with him, so Mr. Nikolaev takes the car back for us. The boy tells us that his name is Ivan. He explains that there are no fences on the farm, so children have to look after the geese and other livestock in the pasture.

After Ivan has taken the geese to their pen, he invites us to his home. It is not as new as some of the village houses nor as old and shabby as some others. The roof is made of straw and the walls are made of thick, sun-dried bricks plastered with mud and whitewashed. Ivan tells us that his cousins on a collective farm in the forest region live in a small log cabin.

We hear a cow mooing and some chickens cackling in a shed at one side of the house. Ivan says that each family in the village is

Village houses in the grassland region have whitewashed walls. Many have thatched roofs.

A farm market. Here farm workers sell fruit and vegetables from their family garden plots.

allowed to raise a few farm animals for their own use or to sell. Every family also has a small garden plot behind their home, where they may raise fruit and vegetables to use as they wish. The people take better care of these little family gardens than they do of the big farm fields. They can sell what they grow here in the market place of a nearby city and keep the money for themselves.

When we go into Ivan's house, we see that it has two rooms, and a cellar for storing food. First we enter the kitchen, which is also used as an everyday living room. A huge stove has been built into the wall that separates this room from the next one. It is made of clay and is neatly whitewashed. In the bottom part is a place for

In a village home. Soviet people often have lace curtains and potted plants in their homes.

the fire, and above that is a huge oven. On top of the stove, high above the fire, is a flat space where members of the family often sleep on cold winter nights. There are electric lights, but no bathroom or running water in the house.

Ivan's grandmother is preparing supper in the kitchen, and she invites us to stay. We go into the next room to wait for Ivan's mother and father to come in from the fields. This is a combination bedroom-living room. There are lace curtains at the windows and pots of garden plants on the sills. On the walls are pictures of Lenin and Khrushchev. In one corner is a small religious picture called an icon. Lace-trimmed bedspreads and huge fluffy pillows decorate the beds. A table and several chairs stand at one side of the room.

For supper we have tomatoes, cucumbers, and steaming soup called borsch. With our meal we eat bread and drink hot tea. The water for our tea is heated in a brass samovar.* (See picture below).

When we get into our car to return to the city, Mr. Nikolaev comes out to say good-by. He and Ivan's family stand and wave to us until our car is out of sight.

DO YOU KNOW

1. Using the pictures in this chapter, describe a Soviet farm village. Describe the inside of a village home.
2. What is a work brigade?
3. Why do children look after farm animals in the pasture?
4. Where may farm workers sell the fruit and vegetables from their family garden plots?

Eating breakfast. Many village homes have only a kitchen and a combination bedroom-living room.

A steel mill in the Ukraine. Soviet mines produce iron ore and other minerals needed by industry.

CHAPTER NINE

NATURAL RESOURCES

The Soviet Union produces most of the raw materials needed by its mills and factories. Within the borders of this enormous country are rich mineral deposits, vast forests, and wide rivers. All of these natural resources are owned by the Soviet government. They are being used to make the Soviet Union a great industrial nation.

Water power. We are standing on the bank of a broad river in the Soviet Union. Upstream, construction workers are building a giant dam and power plant. When this plant is finished, machines called generators will be installed inside. Water from the river will be used to make them run. As they run, the generators will produce hydroelectricity* for factories, farms, and apartment houses.

Water power is one of the Soviet Union's main natural resources, for many great rivers flow through this country. (See map on page 132.) However, until recently very little of this water power was used to produce electricity. It is expensive to build dams and power plants. Also, many of the large rivers are in the

Building a dam on the Angara River. The Soviet government is constructing dams and power plants.

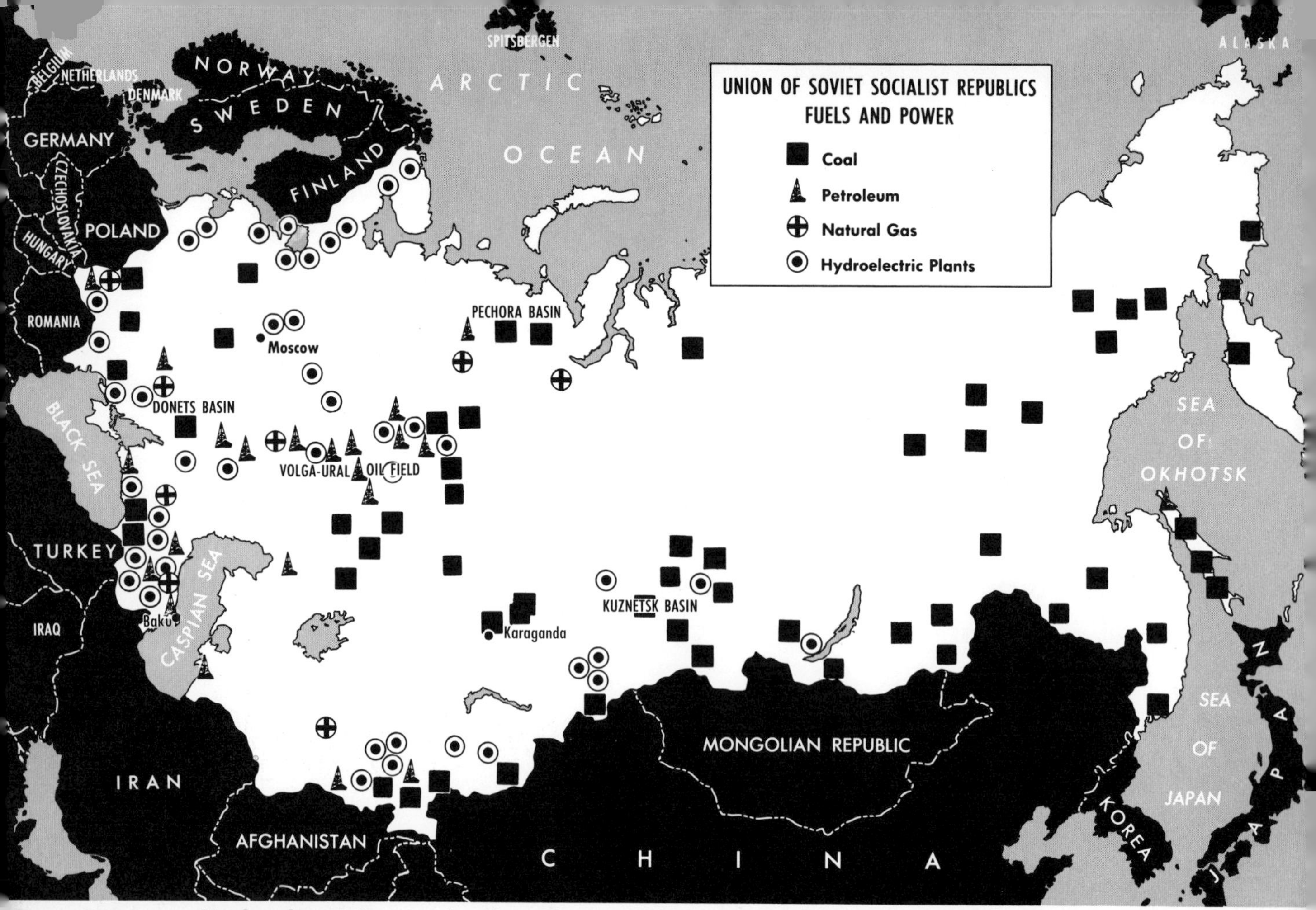

Hydroelectricity, coal, oil, and gas. The Soviet Union is rich in these natural resources.

eastern part of the country, far away from where most of the people live. Today, more and more people are moving eastward, for many new factories are being started in this area. Dams and power plants are being built to supply these industries with power. Miles of power lines are being erected to carry electricity to wherever it is needed.

Coal. Another very important resource needed for industry is coal. The Soviet Union has nearly one fourth of the coal in the world. Some of the most valuable mines are in the Donets Basin, near the Black Sea. (See map above.) They furnish high-grade coal and are close to many manufacturing cities. There is another large coal field near the city of Moscow. However, the soft brown coal dug here does not make a very hot fire.

Most of the other coal fields in the Soviet Union are in remote parts of the country, far away from the main manufacturing cities. The richest of these distant mines is in the Kuznetsk Basin in central Siberia. Another is at Karaganda. Freight trains must travel long distances to carry coal from these far-off mines to factories in the western part of the country.

The Soviet people use coal for many purposes. Large amounts are made into coke,* which is needed to produce iron and steel. A great deal is burned in power plants to heat water and make steam. This steam runs generators which produce electricity.

Mining coal in the Donets Basin. The Soviet Union has nearly a fourth of the world's coal.

Oil derricks near the city of Baku. This is one of the country's main oil fields.

Oil and gas. In addition to coal, the Soviet Union has some of the world's largest deposits of oil and gas. As we look out across the Caspian Sea from the city of Baku, we see tall, black oil derricks in the water. They are pumping oil from wells beneath the sea. Baku is one of the Soviet Union's main oil-producing regions. Even more important than Baku is the Volga-Ural oil field, which lies west of the Ural Mountains. (See map on page 106.) More than a third of the country's oil is produced here.

Trains, tanker ships, and pipelines carry oil from Soviet oil fields to industrial cities in the western part of the country. There it is made into gasoline and other useful products.

The map on page 106 shows where the main gas fields in the Soviet Union are found. Only a small amount of gas is now being used to heat homes and provide fuel for Soviet factories. The Soviet government is planning to increase gas production, however.

Iron ore. Nearly one fourth of the world's iron ore is mined in the Soviet Union. The main Soviet iron mines are at Krivoi Rog and Magnitogorsk. (See map below.) The city of Magnitogorsk received its name because it was built at the foot of a huge mountain of magnetic iron ore. Mine workers here obtain ore from great open pits on the mountain slopes. In the city are enormous blast furnaces and steelworks where the ore is processed to make iron and steel.

It is expensive to make the ore dug at Magnitogorsk into iron and steel, for much of it is full of waste materials. The high-grade ores here have been largely used up. This has happened in several other important iron mines in the Soviet Union.

The Soviet Union produces most of the minerals needed by its mills and factories.

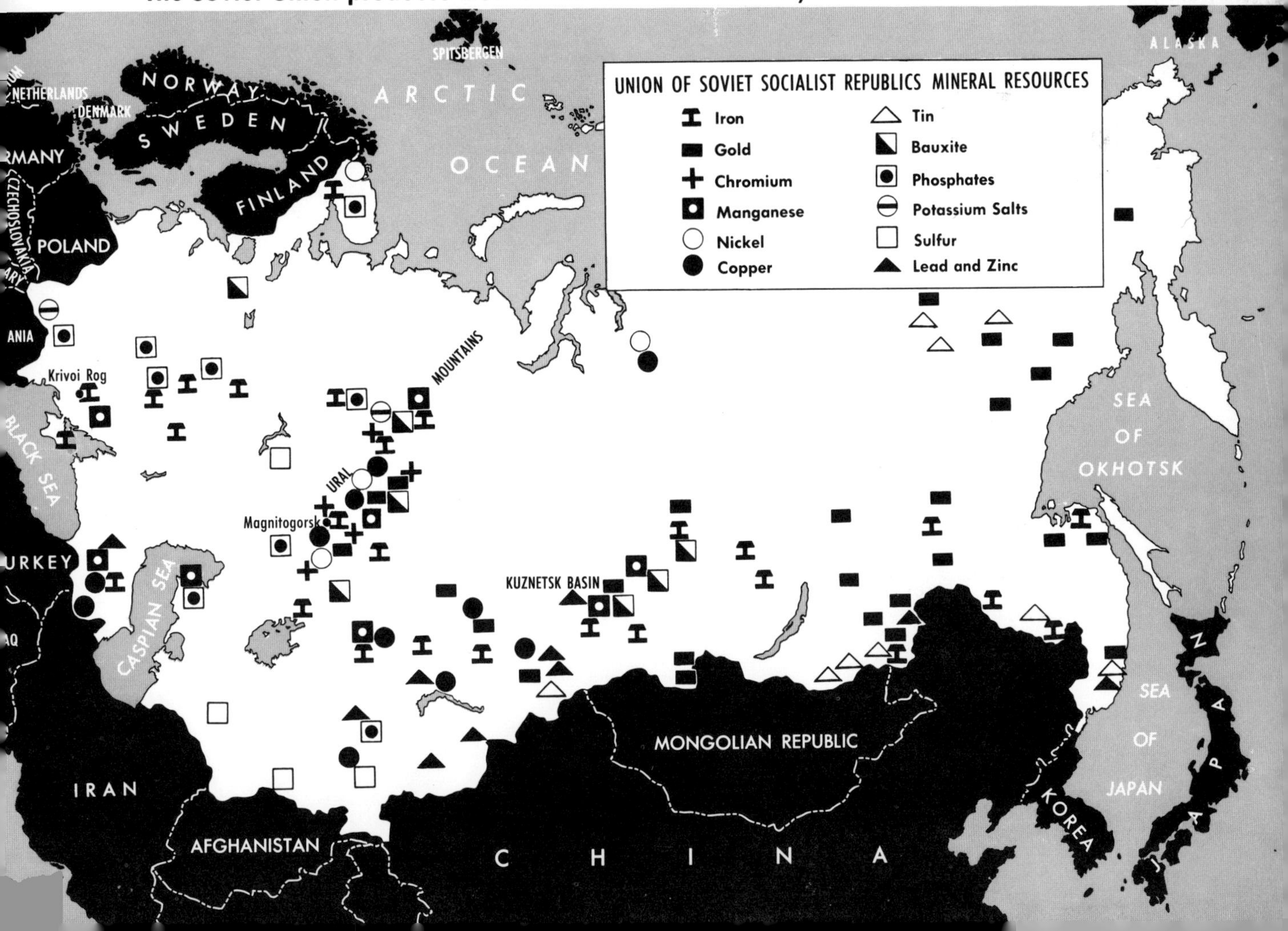

Other minerals. The map on page 109 shows some of the other minerals that are found in the Soviet Union. More manganese is mined here than in any other country. This metal is an important ingredient in making steel. The Soviet Union is also a leading producer of gold and chromium.* There are a few minerals, such as tungsten,* of which the Soviet Union needs a larger supply. Some of these are shipped in from neighboring Communist countries.

Mining manganese in the Ukraine. The Soviet Union produces more manganese than any other country.

A copper mine in Kazakh S.S.R. Ore is mined from open pits and carried away by rail.

Forests. In addition to raw materials taken from mines, Soviet factories use raw materials from the nation's forests. These forests are larger than those of any other country in the world. They stretch in a wide belt from the western border to the Pacific coast. (See map on page 13.)

In the northwest and in some parts of Siberia and the Ural Mountains, there are many lumbering towns. Here we may visit noisy sawmills where logs from the nearby forest are cut into boards. Some of this lumber is sent to factories in Soviet cities, and some is sold to foreign countries.

Floating logs down the Oka River. The Soviet Union has more forests than any other country.

Not all of the logs cut in Soviet forests are processed in the sawmills of small lumbering towns. About a third of the logs are chopped for firewood. Others are sent to factories that make plywood, paper, and wood-chemical products, such as plastics. Thousands more are floated down the Volga River to the sawmills of large industrial cities in the grassland region.

Fishing. Rivers, seas, and lakes provide the Soviet Union with another important natural resource – fish. Japan, China, and the United States are the only countries that catch more fish than the Soviet Union each year.

One fourth of the Soviet Union's fish comes from the Pacific Ocean. Near the coast lie rich salmon-fishing grounds. Soviet fishing fleets also sail to the North Pacific and the Antarctic to hunt for seals and whales.

Many fish are caught in the Barents Sea, which borders the Soviet Union on the northwest. (See map on page 10.) Fishermen from the port of Murmansk and other northern coastal towns bring in large catches of cod, haddock, and herring from this sea.

The richest inland fishing waters in the Soviet Union are in the Caspian Sea. One of the most interesting kinds of fish found here is sturgeon. Some of these fish grow to be more than eight feet long. Fishermen often catch the sturgeon before they lay their eggs. The eggs look like masses of tiny black beads, and are called caviar. The Soviet people consider caviar to be a very delicious food.

Weighing a sturgeon. Only Japan, China, and the United States catch more fish than the Soviet Union.

Furs. During the winter months, trappers in the lonely woodlands in the eastern part of the Soviet Union set their traps for fur-bearing animals. Other trappers work farther north in the bleak tundra. The thick, soft pelts of silver fox, sable,* and ermine* which they obtain are sold in many foreign countries.

DO YOU KNOW

1. Using the maps on pages 106 and 109, name some of the natural resources obtained from Soviet mines.
2. What is the Soviet Union doing to make better use of its water power?
3. How do Soviet forests compare in size with those of other countries?
4. Tell about the Soviet fishing industry.

Furs from the northern and eastern parts of the Soviet Union are sold in many countries.

Measuring a turbine shaft. The Soviet Union is second only to the United States in manufacturing.

CHAPTER TEN
INDUSTRY

The Soviet Union wants to become the world's leading industrial country. Sixty years ago it was in fifth place among the industrial nations of the world. The United States, the United Kingdom, France, and Germany produced more manufactured goods each year. Today, only the United States is still ahead of the Soviet Union. The graph on page 117 shows us how far ahead the United States is.

The Soviet people suffer so that new industries can be built. The Soviet people have been forced to go without many things they need in order that their country may build new industries. When we walk through a department store in Moscow, we notice that many of the goods for sale are very expensive. If a Soviet man wanted to buy one of the ordinary suits we see here, both he and his wife would have to save for more than seven months to have enough money to pay for it. In the United States, however, a family would need to save for only one and a half months before the father could buy himself a suit. This is because clothes are cheaper and wages are higher in the United States.

A display of kitchen utensils. Household goods and clothes are very expensive in the Soviet Union.

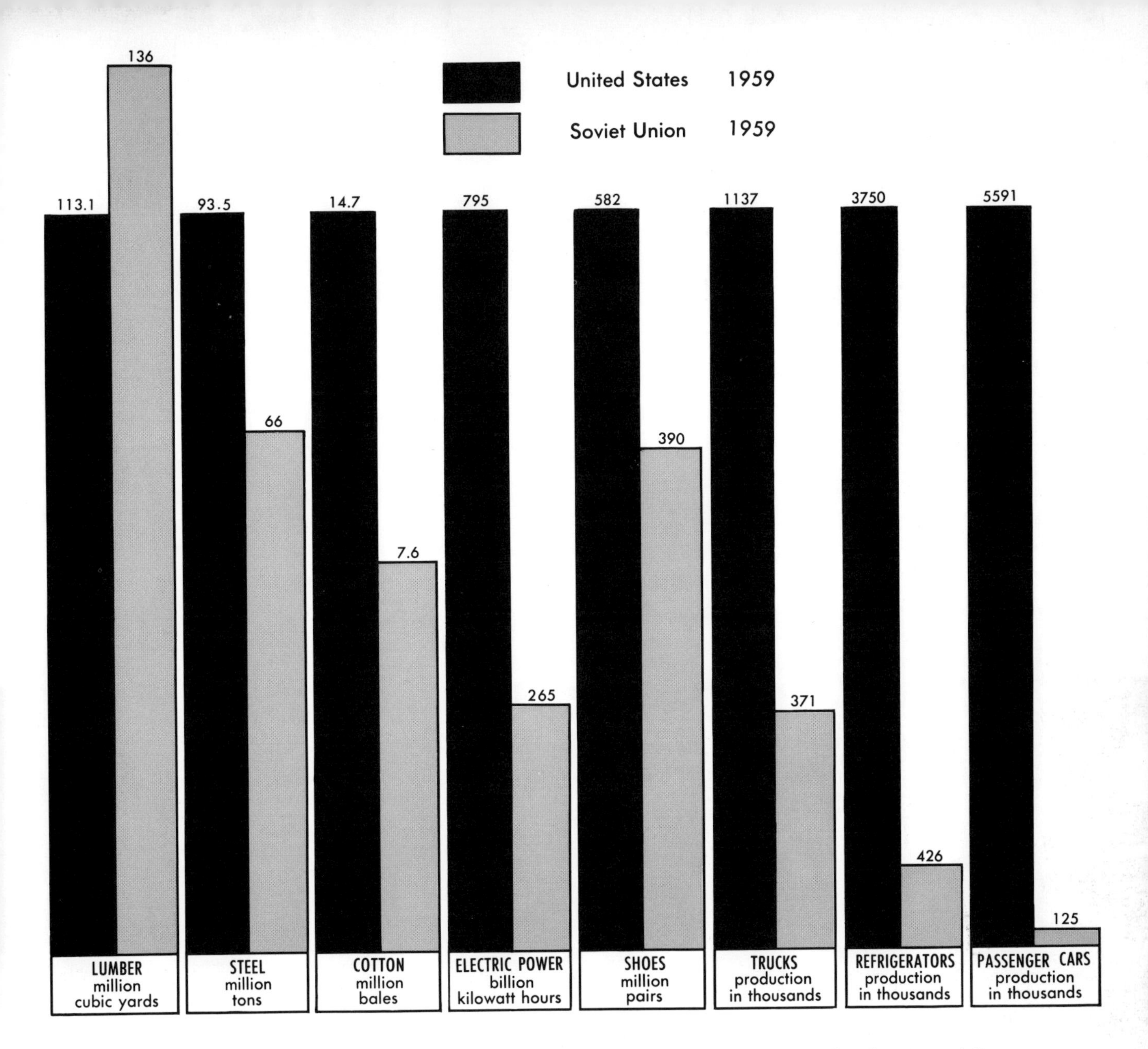

American and Soviet industry compared. The Soviet Union wants to overtake the United States.

There is a special reason why clothing and household goods are so expensive in the Soviet Union. The nation's leaders do not want many factories to produce these articles. They want to use the country's factory workers and raw materials to make mining equipment, electric generators, and other heavy machinery. These can be used to start new factories, mines, and power plants, which will help the Soviet Union catch up with the United States.

Assembling automobiles in a Moscow factory. All industries are owned by the government.

All Soviet industry is controlled by the government. The Soviet leaders can decide what factories will produce because all the country's industries are owned by the government. A special government committee plans how many new industries are to be built and just exactly what is to be produced. Then the people are expected to carry out these plans. If you will go back to page 52 and read about the Five-Year Plans, you will learn more about how the Soviet Union became a great industrial country.

The metal industry. In the last thirty years, the government has built many blast furnaces and mills to make iron and steel. Today, the Soviet Union produces more iron and steel each year than any country in the world except the United States.

A great deal of coal is needed to smelt* iron ore. For this reason, many iron and steel centers are located near the coal fields in the Donets Basin and the Kuznetsk Basin. (Compare maps on pages 106 and 120.) Others have been built near the large deposits of iron ore in the Ural Mountains. The most important iron and steel center in the Urals is Magnitogorsk.

A tractor plant. The Soviet metal industry produces mainly heavy machinery and military equipment.

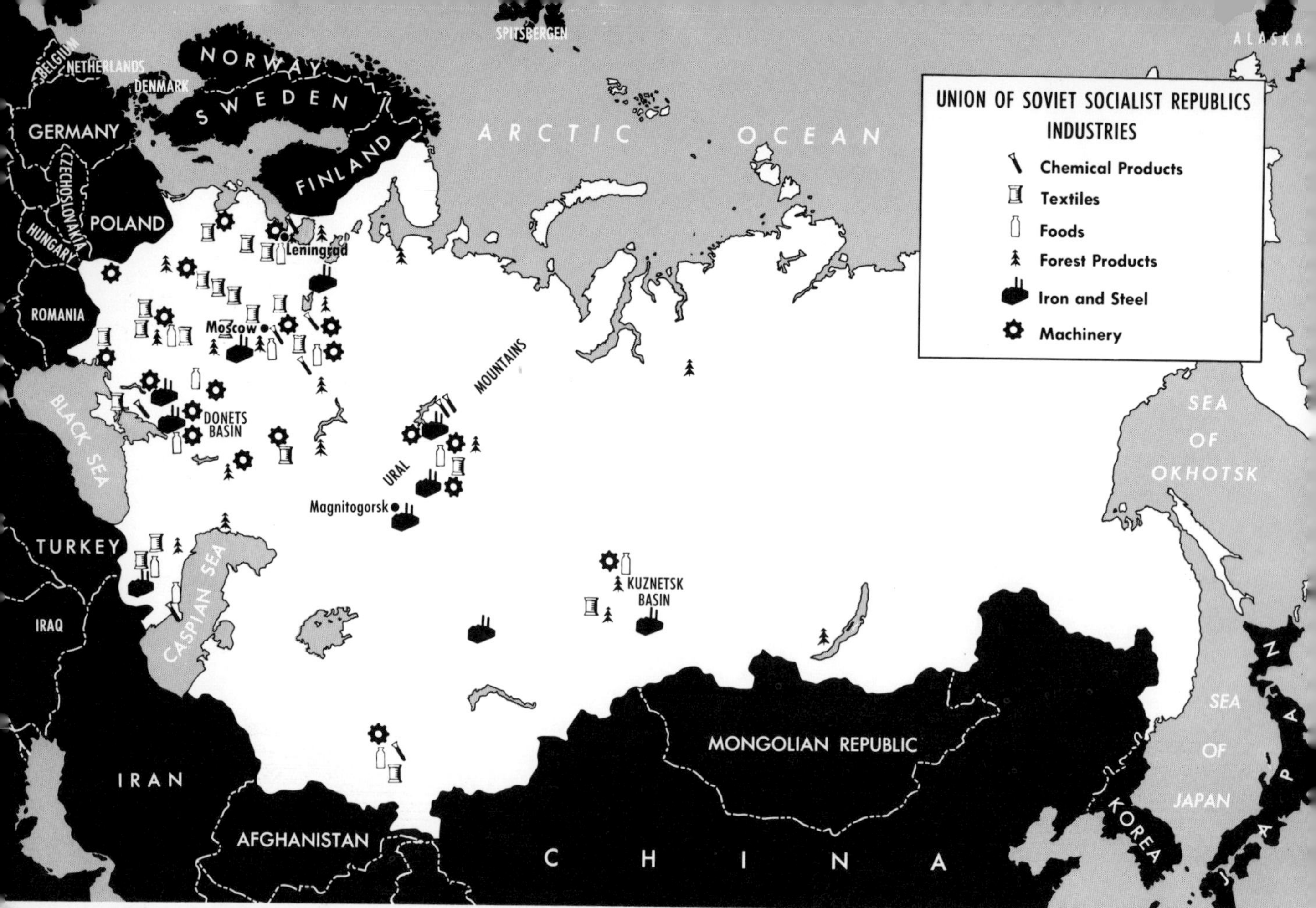

Industries in the Soviet Union are located mainly in the western part of the country.

Freight trains carry bars of iron and steel from Soviet iron and steel mills to factories that make metal goods. The map above shows us that most of these factories are in the western part of the country.

Most Soviet metal factories make heavy equipment, such as mining machinery, railroad cars, and electric-power generators. Many of them produce the huge machines that are used to make equipment for new factories. Large numbers of jet airplanes, tanks, and other military equipment are also manufactured.

The chemical industry. The Soviet government has also built many chemical plants. (See map above.) Some of these use raw materials from the country's mines. When we visit one plant, we see workers making fertilizers out of phosphate* rocks. In another, we watch sulfur* being processed to make insect killers and explosives. In a third, workers are making dyes from a black, sticky material called coal* tar.

There are large refineries near the oil fields of Baku and in many industrial cities. Here crude oil is refined to make gasoline and other fuels. Some of the waste materials left when this is done are used in making synthetic rubber. Larger quantities of synthetic rubber, however, are made from potatoes.

Pumping oil into tank cars. The Soviet Union has some of the world's largest oil deposits.

A chemical plant in Saratov. Waste gases from an oil refinery are used to produce alcohol.

Soviet forests also furnish raw materials for chemical plants and paper mills. Logs are cut into chips and cooked with chemicals to make pulp for paper. Plastics, turpentine, and alcohol are also made from forest products.

The Soviet chemical industry has grown very much in recent years, but it still does not provide the people with all the chemical products they need. However, the government is planning to build new chemical plants.

The textile industry. In the southern part of the Soviet Union are many new cotton mills. Here workers tend whirring machines that spin cotton into thread. Power looms weave this thread into cloth. The cotton used in these mills is grown in nearby fields. (See map on page 92.)

Making cotton cloth is the most important branch of the Soviet textile industry. The oldest cotton mills are in the northern part of the country, near the cities of Moscow and Ivanovo. Fifty years ago, these mills had to import from other countries nearly half of the cotton they used. Now, however, the Soviet Union grows all the cotton it needs.

In addition to cotton mills, the Soviet Union has other textile mills that make woolen, linen, silk, and rayon cloth. In garment

A knitting machine. Manufacturing cotton goods is the main branch of the Soviet textile industry.

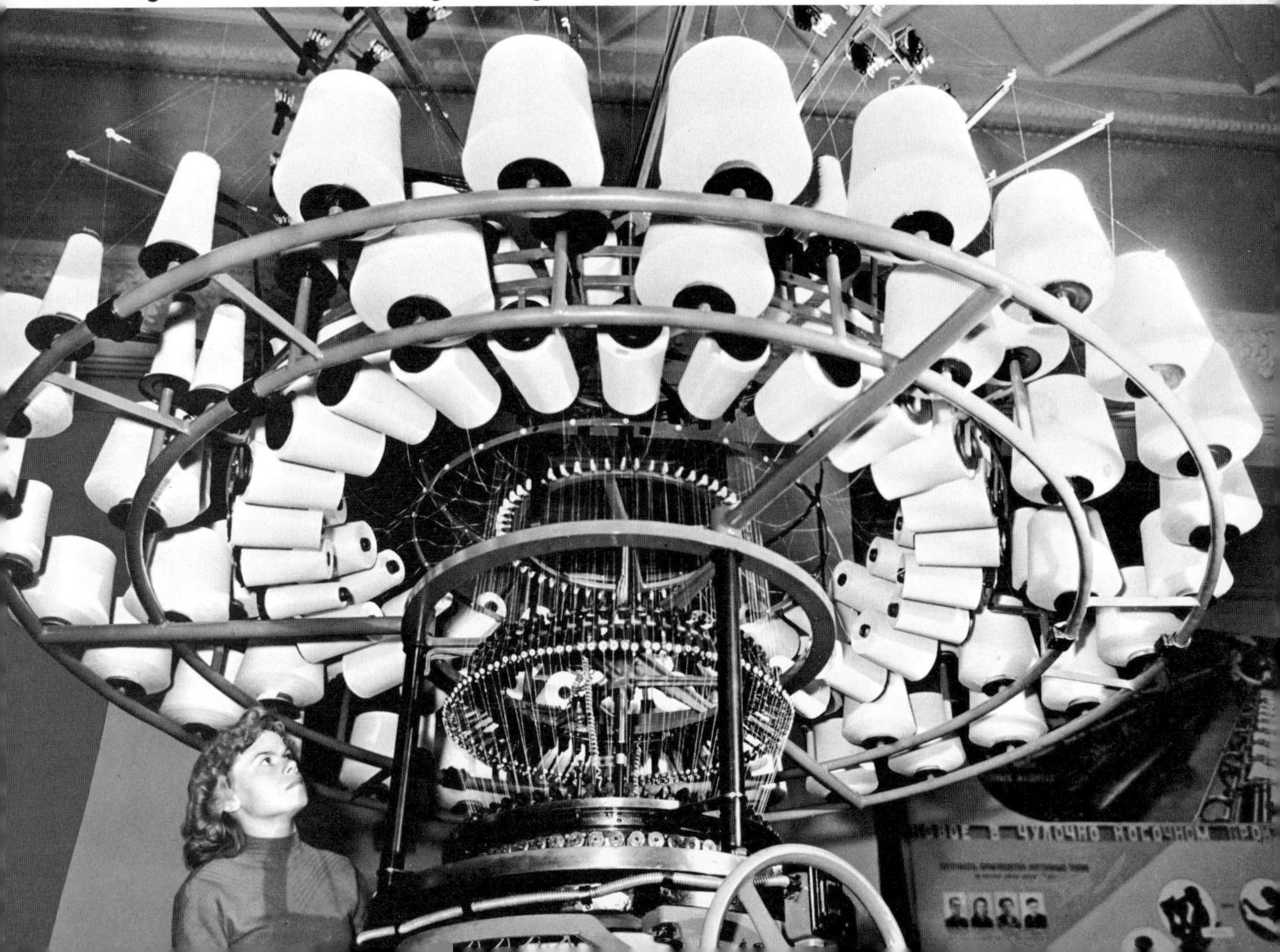

factories, workers make this cloth into clothing. The Soviet people, however, want more clothing than these factories can furnish.

Many Soviet manufactured goods are poorly made. Many articles made in Soviet factories are of poor quality. Clothes usually do not fit well, paint comes off when you touch it, and electric light bulbs burn out soon after you buy them. One reason for this is that workers often rush to produce as much as the government orders them to.

There is another reason why many Soviet goods are of poor quality. In the United States, a man who invents a new kind of paint can borrow money and start a factory to manufacture it. If it is good paint, people will buy it and he will be successful. If not, he will go out of business, for they will buy better paint made in some other man's factory. In the Soviet Union, this man could not start his own factory. He would have to take his formula for paint to the government. If the leaders wanted to, they could order the government paint factories to make it. However, they might not want to make a change at that time. They know that people will buy the poorer paint the factories are already making because it is almost the only kind there is.

The Soviet people are beginning to show that they are tired of buying poorly made goods. The leaders know that they cannot let the people become too dissatisfied, so they are showing more interest in improving the quality of manufactured articles.

Some Soviet products are very well made. There are some products which are made with great care in the Soviet Union. The government pays high salaries to scientists and engineers who design jet airplanes and other military equipment. They are given all the money and materials necessary to make scientific discoveries needed to produce rockets and man-made satellites.*

Altogether, the Soviet leaders spend nearly one fourth of their nation's money on things needed for war. This helps us to realize how anxious the Soviet Union is to become the world's most powerful nation.

DO YOU KNOW

1. Why don't the Soviet people have all the clothes they want? Why are many manufactured goods poorly made?
2. On the map on page 120, find the iron and steel centers. How does the Soviet Union rank in steel production?
3. What is the main branch of the textile industry? Where is it centered?

A nuclear research center. The Soviet Union wants to become the world's most powerful country.

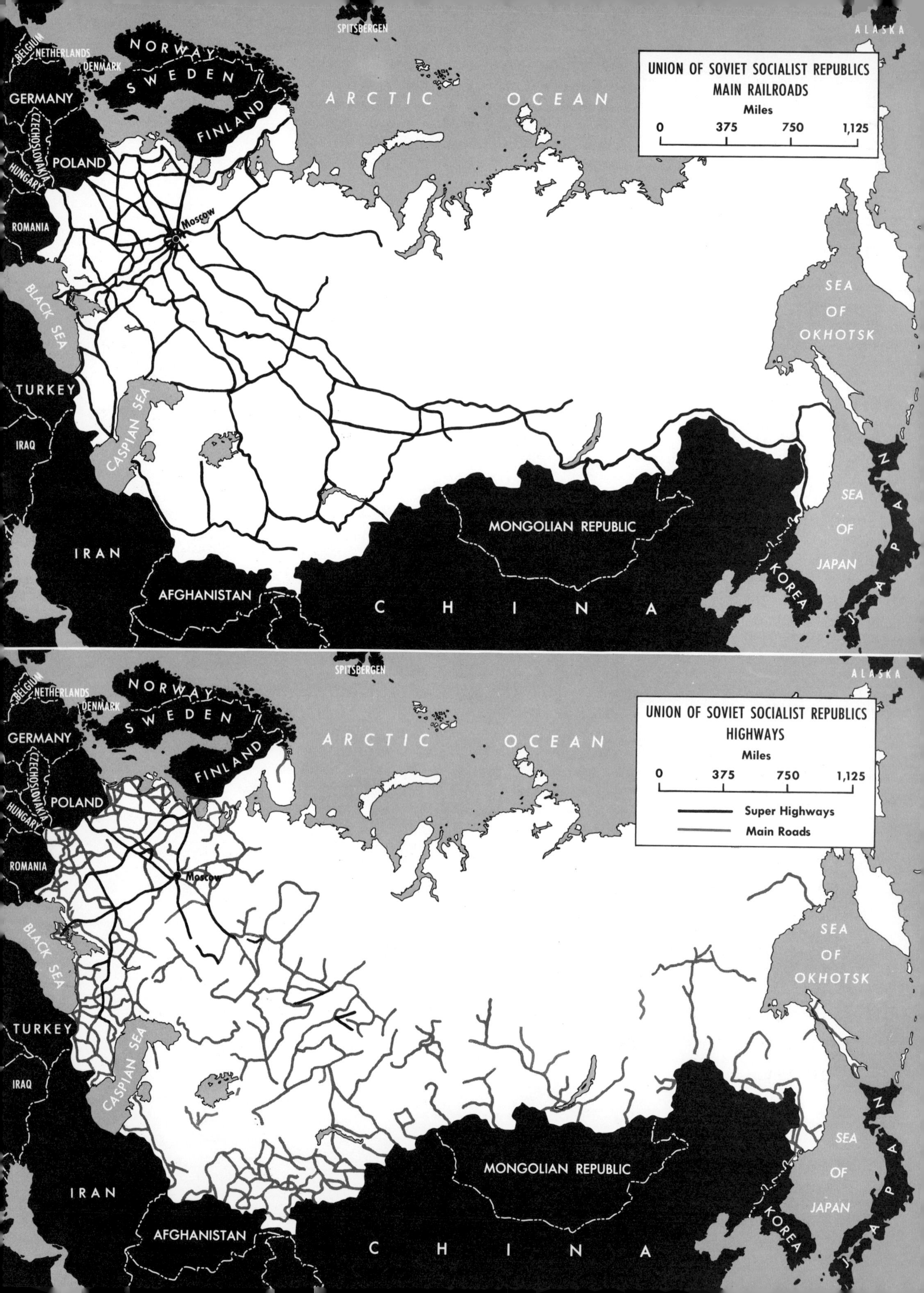
SPITSBERGEN
ALASKA
UNION OF SOVIET SOCIALIST REPUBLICS
MAIN RAILROADS
Miles
0
375
750
1,125
BELGIUM
NETHERLANDS
DENMARK
NORWAY
SWEDEN
FINLAND
GERMANY
CZECHOSLOVAKIA
POLAND
HUNGARY
ROMANIA
ARCTIC OCEAN
Moscow
BLACK SEA
TURKEY
CASPIAN SEA
IRAQ
IRAN
AFGHANISTAN
MONGOLIAN REPUBLIC
CHINA
KOREA
SEA OF OKHOTSK
SEA OF JAPAN
JAPAN
SPITSBERGEN
ALASKA
UNION OF SOVIET SOCIALIST REPUBLICS
HIGHWAYS
Miles
0
375
750
1,125
Super Highways
Main Roads
BELGIUM
NETHERLANDS
DENMARK
NORWAY
SWEDEN
FINLAND
GERMANY
CZECHOSLOVAKIA
POLAND
HUNGARY
ROMANIA
ARCTIC OCEAN
Moscow
BLACK SEA
TURKEY
CASPIAN SEA
IRAQ
IRAN
AFGHANISTAN
MONGOLIAN REPUBLIC
CHINA
KOREA
SEA OF OKHOTSK
SEA OF JAPAN
JAPAN

A railroad yard in Moscow. Many trains in the Soviet Union are now powered by electricity.

CHAPTER ELEVEN

TRANSPORTATION AND COMMUNICATION

A train ride across the Soviet Union. The winter wind whistles around our ears as we hurry through the port city of Leningrad to the railroad station. In just a half an hour we will begin our journey across the Soviet Union to the Pacific port of Vladivostok. The trip will take us at least nine days, for Vladivostok is more than six thousand miles away. To reach this distant city, we will travel over the longest railroad in the world, the Trans-Siberian Railway.

Soviet railroads and highways are mainly in the western part of the country. All railroads are owned by the government.

To catch the Trans-Siberian express train, we must travel from Leningrad to Moscow. Since this will take all night, we have made reservations on a type of railroad car called a wagon-lit.* It has a number of private compartments opening onto an aisle that extends along one side of the car. When the white-coated attendant shows us to our compartment, we find that it has two comfortable berths and a small washroom. As we take off our coats, the train jerks into motion, and we are on our way.

In the morning, we reach Moscow and transfer our luggage to the train that will take us to Vladivostok. On this train we travel "soft class," which means that our compartment has four comfortable berths. Most passengers on the Trans-Siberian Railway cannot afford to travel this way. Instead, they ride in "hard-class" compartments, which have hard slabs of wood for bunks.

Our train moves slowly out of the station, and soon we are riding through the snow-covered countryside. When we stop at a station, many of the passengers get out to stretch their legs and buy a little food. They buy cheese or salami and black bread. They also get hot water to make tea. The Russian passengers in our compartment have brought large bundles of food with them, which they share with us. Though there is a dining car on the train, the meals are not very good and many people prefer to bring their own food.

A geography teacher in our compartment invites us to look at his map of Soviet railways. Here we see that the Trans-Siberian is the only railroad reaching across the eastern part of the country. There are no transcontinental highways in the Soviet Union. Neither are there any rivers that flow all the way across this vast land. Therefore, the railroad is the main link between the Pacific coast and the western parts of the country.

On the map, we see that there are many railroads in the western part of the country, where most of the people live. Many of these railroads lead into Moscow. In fact, the rail network around Moscow looks like a giant spider web, with the capital at the center. Altogether, we are told, there are about 75,000 miles of railroad track in the Soviet Union. This seems like a great deal, but it is only about a third as much as the United States has. The Soviet government owns all the railways and is planning to lay more track.

A passenger train. Railroads are the most important means of transportation in the Soviet Union.

The geography teacher tells us that railroads are the most important means of transportation in the Soviet Union. They carry more than four fifths of all the freight and passengers in the country. As we cross western Siberia, we see freight cars hauling coal from remote mining districts to factories in the cities. These factories could not operate unless the railroads brought them raw materials.

Roads and highways. Except when our train pulls into big cities, we do not see paved roads in the eastern part of the Soviet Union.

A village road. Most of the roads in the Soviet Union are unpaved. In rainy weather they are muddy.

Moscow streets. Few Soviet people own automobiles. Most city people ride buses or streetcars.

Even in the cities, many of the streets are unpaved. Most of the country roads we see through the train window are really just dirt tracks leading from villages to the railroad.

Most of the paved roads in the Soviet Union are in the western part of the country. They are usually two lanes wide and link Moscow to other large Soviet cities. These roads are used mainly by trucks and buses.

Automobiles are scarce and expensive in the Soviet Union, and very few people own them. Most city workers go to and from their jobs in buses or streetcars. Peasants coming in from the countryside ride in trucks or walk.

Water travel in the Soviet Union. Our train trip across the Soviet Union ends as we pull into the port city of Vladivostok. The day after we arrive, we walk down to the Vladivostok water front. On this cold winter day, huge icebreakers are cracking the ice in the harbor to permit ships to enter and leave the port. A passer-by tells us that many Soviet harbors are frozen from four to nine months each year.

During the months when the ice is melted, Soviet ships carry freight from port to port within the country. There is little water traffic between the Soviet Union and other countries, however. In summer, some vessels use the Northern Sea Route along the Arctic coast of the Soviet Union. Others sail across the Black and Caspian seas that lie to the south. Ships also travel on the many great rivers that flow through the Soviet Union. The most important of these

Rivers and canals in the Soviet Union. The Volga River is the most important water highway.

The Moscow Canal links the Moskva and the Volga rivers. Canals have made Moscow an important port.

rivers is the mighty Volga, in the western part of the country. (See map on opposite page.)

The Soviet people have dug many canals to connect their country's rivers and to link them to the surrounding seas. Among the most important of these is the Moscow Canal, between the Moskva River and the Volga. Another is the great canal that connects the

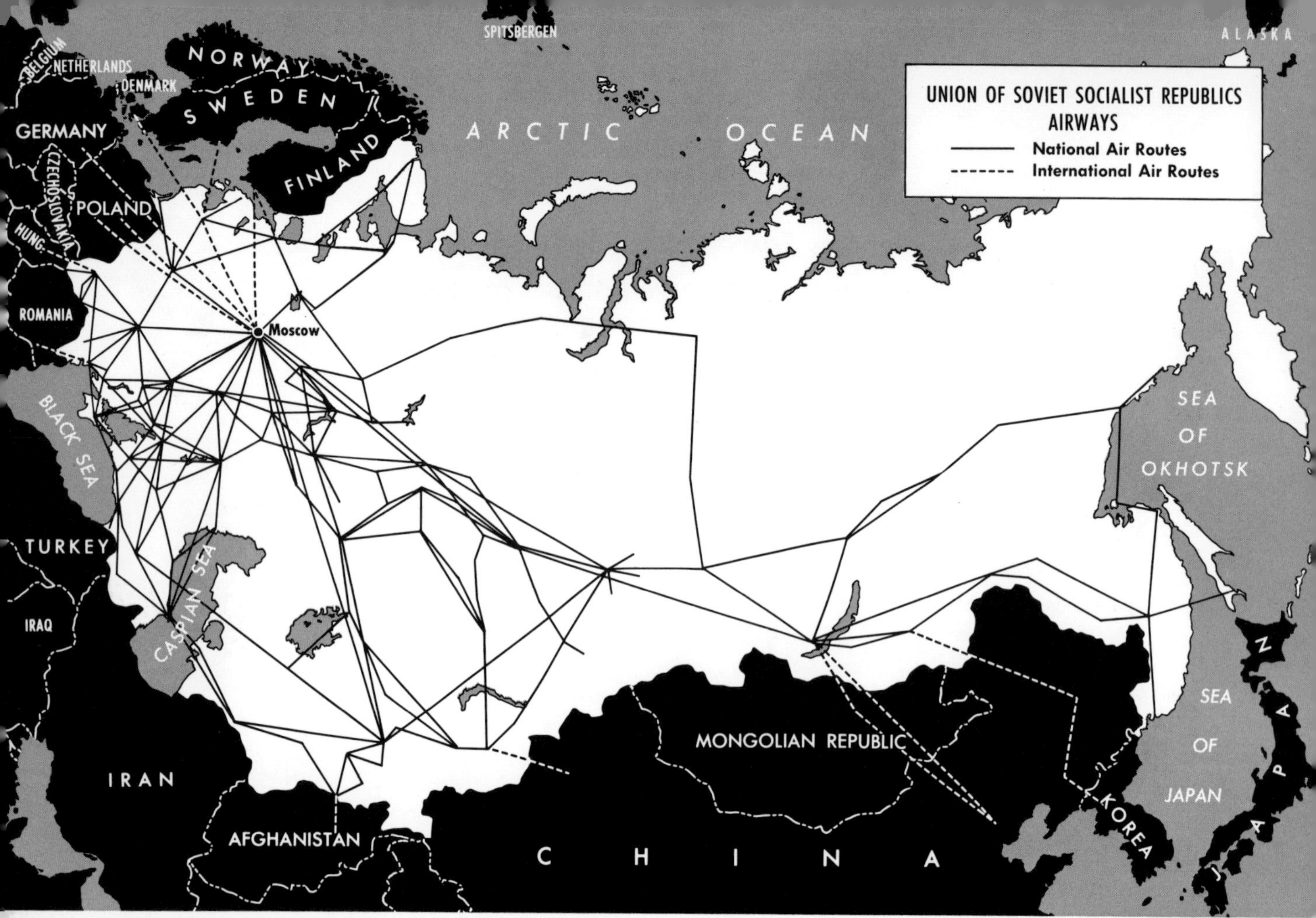

Soviet air routes. In a country as large as the Soviet Union, air travel is very important.

Volga and Don rivers. (See map on page 132.) Because of man-made waterways such as these, the inland city of Moscow has become an important port. Ships can come to Moscow along rivers and canals from the Black, Caspian, White, and Baltic seas. (See maps on pages 10 and 132.)

Air travel. In a country as huge as the Soviet Union, air travel is very important. Air routes link all the large cities and many of the smaller ones. (See map above.) There is only one airline in the Soviet Union. It is called Aeroflot and is owned by the government. Many of Aeroflot's passenger planes are new jets that can travel at speeds of more than five hundred miles an hour. Aeroflot planes fly to important cities in many countries of the world, but foreign planes are permitted to land at only four Soviet airports.

Communications. In the Soviet Union, people can hear, see, and read about only those items of news and interest which the government wishes them to know. All movies and newspapers are checked, or censored, to make sure they do not criticize the government. Radio and television programs are also censored. Many families have radio sets. The government has also placed loudspeakers along the streets, in the parks, and on the trains. The government uses these to broadcast music and the news it wants the people to hear. There are more than two and a half million television sets in the Soviet Union, but this is only about one twentieth as many as there are in the United States.

An Aeroflot jet plane. Aeroflot is the Soviet Union's only airline. It is owned by the government.

People in the Soviet Union keep in touch with each other by mail, telephone, and telegraph. Phones are scarce, and not every family has one. On a holiday, it is customary for Soviet people to send each other telegrams of good wishes.

DO YOU KNOW

1. Use the maps on page 126 to explain why the Trans-Siberian Railway is important.
2. What kind of traffic do you usually see on roads in the Soviet Union?
3. Explain how the inland city of Moscow has become an important port.
4. What is an important difference between Soviet and American newspapers?

A television studio. Television and radio stations in the Soviet Union are run by the government.

The city of Moscow lies on the Moskva River. It is the Soviet Union's capital and largest city.

CHAPTER TWELVE

CITIES

Moscow. In the center of the wide plain that stretches through the western part of the Soviet Union lies one of the world's most interesting cities. This is Moscow, the nation's capital and the home of more than five million people. (See map on page 147.)

It is the morning of May 1 when we begin our tour of Moscow. Our guide, whose name is Volodia, tells us that this is an important Soviet holiday, similar to our Labor Day. Later this morning

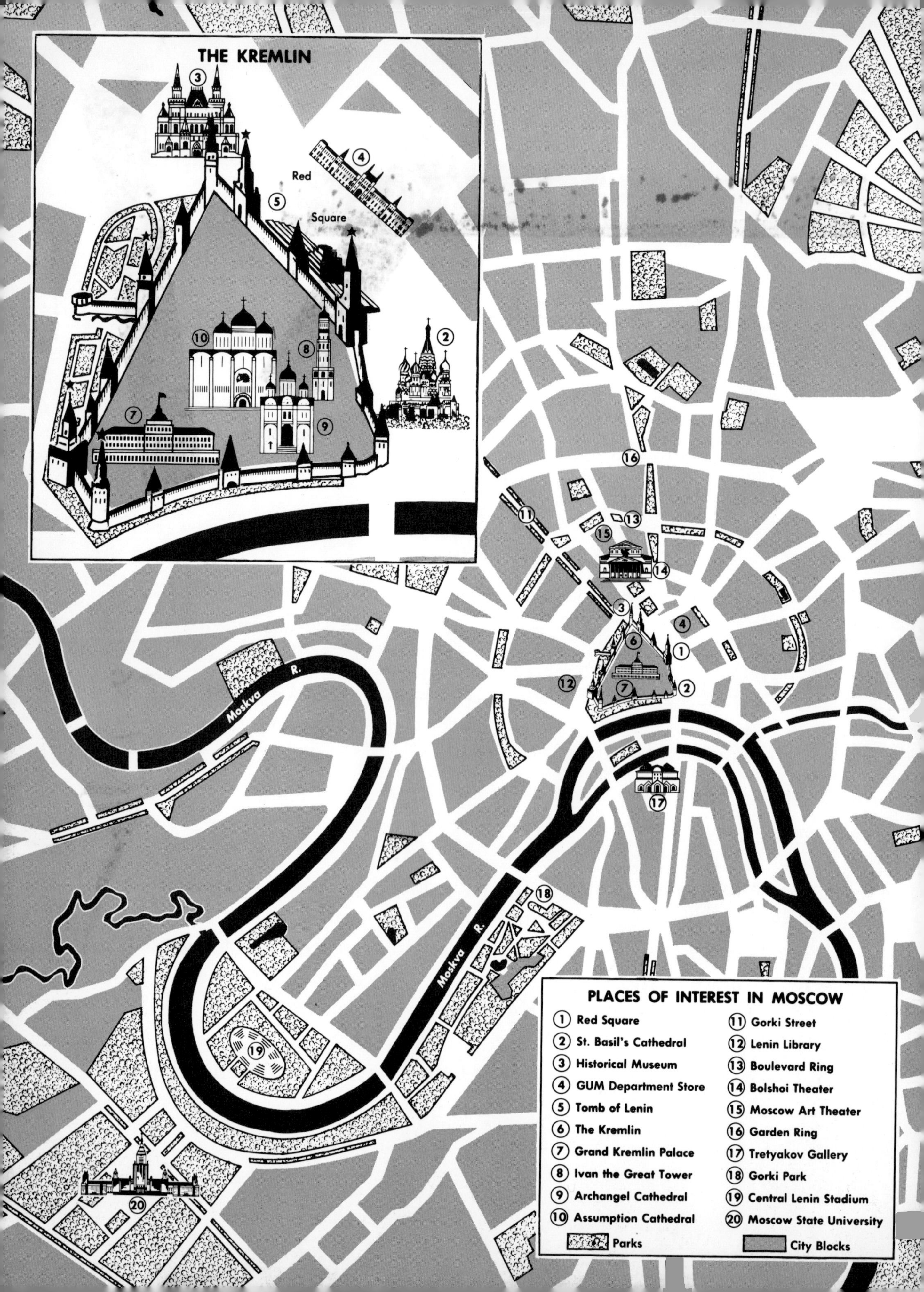
THE KREMLIN
Red
Square
Moskva R.
Moskva R.
PLACES OF INTEREST IN MOSCOW
1 Red Square
2 St. Basil's Cathedral
3 Historical Museum
4 GUM Department Store
5 Tomb of Lenin
6 The Kremlin
7 Grand Kremlin Palace
8 Ivan the Great Tower
9 Archangel Cathedral
10 Assumption Cathedral
11 Gorki Street
12 Lenin Library
13 Boulevard Ring
14 Bolshoi Theater
15 Moscow Art Theater
16 Garden Ring
17 Tretyakov Gallery
18 Gorki Park
19 Central Lenin Stadium
20 Moscow State University
Parks
City Blocks

Moscow is located in the center of the wide plain that stretches through the western part of the country. In the heart of the city is Red Square.

a great parade will pass through Red Square, which lies in the center of the city. This square is located on a hill overlooking the Moskva River, which winds through the heart of Moscow.

When we arrive at Red Square, we see why it was chosen as the parade grounds. It is a vast, open space more than a half mile long, paved with cobblestones. Red and white lines have been painted on the ground to help the people in parades march in straight rows.

While we wait for the parade to begin, we look around at the buildings that face Red Square. At the southeastern end stands an ancient church that looks almost as though it were crowned

Red Square is a huge, open space more than one-half mile long. Large parades are held here.

St. Basil's Cathedral has nine towers topped by brightly painted domes. Religious services are no longer held in this ancient church.

with giant swirls of bright-colored candy. This is St. Basil's Cathedral, now used as a museum. It has nine towers topped by onion-shaped domes, which are painted in designs of red, yellow, green, and glistening gold. At the northwestern end of the square stands a dignified red brick building. This is the Historical Museum. Along the eastern side of the square stretches GUM, the largest department store in the Soviet Union. It is owned by the government. Today it is decorated with red banners bearing Communist slogans and large pictures of Marx and Lenin. On the western side of Red Square stand two of the most famous structures in the Soviet Union. One is the tomb of Lenin. It is made of polished dark-red granite and is shaped somewhat like a flat-topped pyramid. The other is an ancient fortress called the Kremlin, which is now the center of the Soviet Union's government.

The GUM Department Store is on the eastern side of Red Square. It is owned by the government.

Boats passing the Kremlin. The city of Moscow grew up around this ancient fortress.

The Kremlin is surrounded by a high wall about one and a half miles around. (See map on page 138.) Along the top of the wall rise high watchtowers. Five of them are topped with huge red stars that glow at night. Inside the walls are several pale-yellow palaces and four cathedrals, in which church services are no longer held. The golden domes of the cathedrals glitter in the sun. Some of the buildings in the Kremlin are used by the main governing bodies of the Soviet Union. Others are now museums. People from all over the country visit these museums to see the jewels, crowns, golden dishes, and robes that were used by Russia's early rulers.

The Kremlin stands on the spot where Moscow first began. More than eight hundred years ago, when the country was divided among quarreling princes, one prince built a wooden fortress here. The town that grew up around the fortress became the city of

Moscow. In time, the princes of Moscow united the people under their rule, and Moscow became the capital of Russia.

The great parade is beginning now. First come ranks of soldiers and lines of tanks and other military equipment. Then come rows of workers, athletes, and students. The government expects factories, universities, and Party groups to send people to march in parades.

When the parade is over, Volodia takes us to see other parts of Moscow. There are twelve wide streets that branch out from the

Gorki Street leads northwestward from Red Square. It is a broad, tree-lined thoroughfare.

Kremlin. We go up Gorki Street, a broad, tree-lined thoroughfare that leads northwestward. (See map on page 138.) On both sides of the street are stores, restaurants, and bookshops. The sidewalks are crowded with people.

After crossing several busy streets, we come to a broad avenue called Boulevard Ring. This avenue runs in a giant circle around the Kremlin. (See map on page 138.) When Moscow was very small, a high wall surrounding the city stood here, but it was torn down as the city grew larger. Most of Moscow's restaurants, stores, government offices, and theaters are in the part of the city that lies inside Boulevard Ring. The most famous theater is the beautiful Bolshoi, with its eight white pillars crowned by a cluster of statues.

About a half mile beyond Boulevard Ring, Gorki Street crosses another wide avenue that circles the Kremlin. This is Garden Ring. (See map on page 138.) Like Boulevard Ring, it has taken the place of a wall that once surrounded the city. Along the wide thoroughfares and narrow cobblestone streets that lie between these two circling avenues are many old mansions that have been turned into apartment houses. Right beside them are new apartment houses and shabby little wooden cottages. Seven towering skyscrapers have also been built along Garden Ring.

Volodia tells us that the city stretches on for many miles outside Garden Ring. There are more homes and apartment houses there, as well as hundreds of factories, for Moscow is the country's main industrial city. Eleven huge railroad stations and several large parks and stadiums are also located in that part of the city. In the cool, green birch woods that surround Moscow are the pleasant country homes of important Communist officials and other wealthy people.

Now Volodia suggests that we take a subway out to the Agricultural Fairgrounds that lie at the northern edge of the city. The subway station looks almost like a palace, for it is very large and is decorated with many paintings and statues. When we reach the Fairgrounds, we see that they are also very elaborate. In the center is a large fountain surrounded by carefully shaped flower beds. On the grounds are buildings where farm products grown in different parts of the country are displayed.

Next we take a subway to the southern part of the city to see two interesting places that lie across the Moskva River. First we visit the Tretyakov Gallery, where many beautiful paintings are hung.

The Agricultural Fairgrounds are located at the northern edge of Moscow.

Then we go to Moscow State University, which stands on a hill overlooking the river. Volodia's brother attends classes in a towering white building that is the main part of this great university.

Leningrad. Now we fly four hundred miles northwestward to Leningrad, the second largest city in the Soviet Union. (See map on opposite page.) This important port city is built along the Neva River where it flows into the Gulf of Finland. It was founded more than 250 years ago by Peter the Great, one of the nation's best-known rulers. For about two hundred years before the Communist Revolution, this city was called St. Petersburg and was the country's capital. Today, about three million people live here. Many of them earn their living as factory workers, for this is an important industrial center.

Leningrad is the Soviet Union's second largest city. It is an important port.

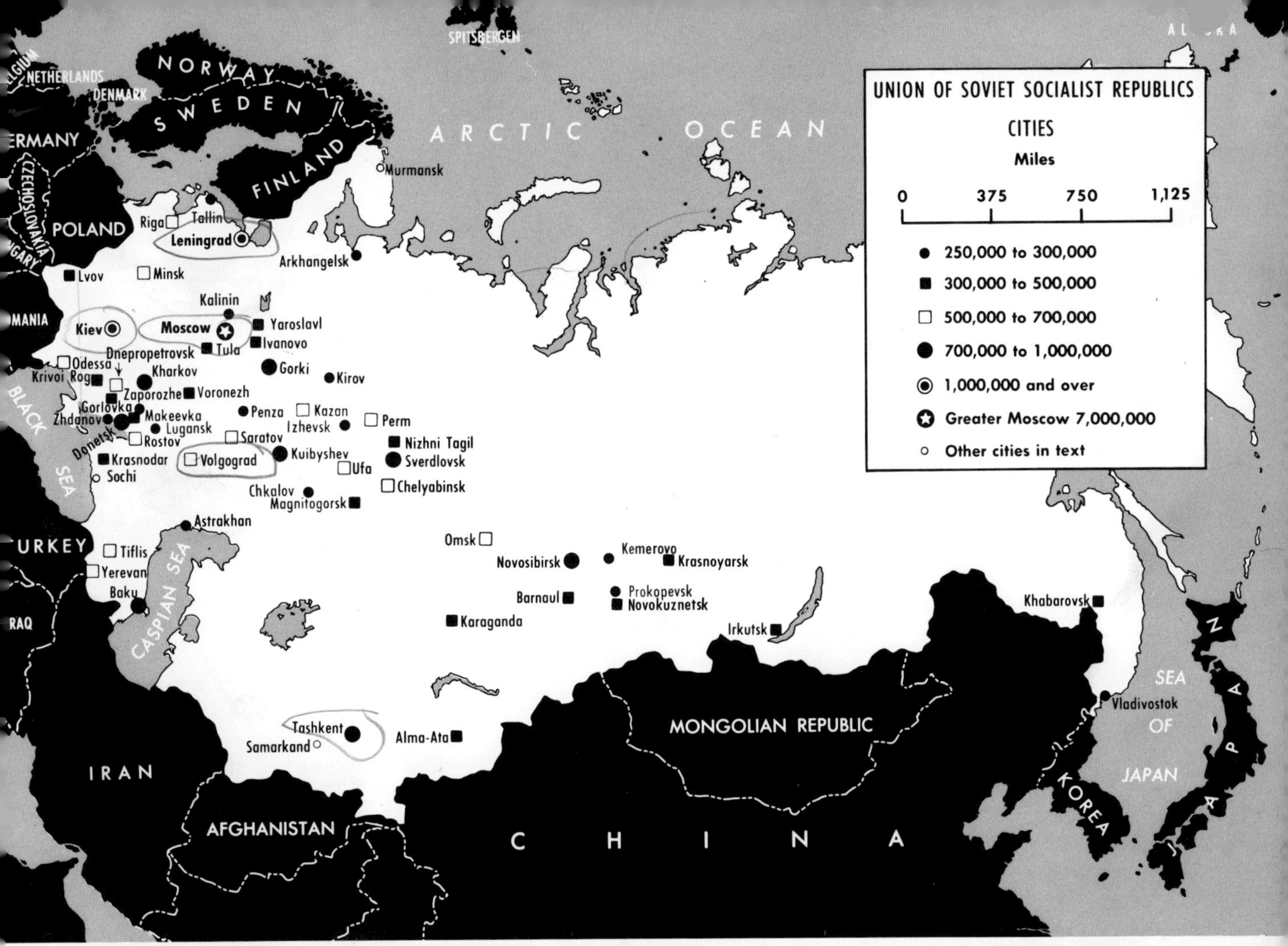

The Soviet Union has many large cities. Most of them are in the western half of the country.

We spend several days touring Leningrad. As we walk through the city streets, we see several canals crossed by graceful bridges. We walk along one of the canals until we come to the Neva River, which flows through the city. An enormous statue of Peter the Great stands on the riverbank. On an island in the river rises the slender spire of a gray stone building called Peter and Paul Fortress.

There are many museums and art galleries in Leningrad. Some of these were once palaces. The Museum of the Revolution, formerly called the Winter Palace, was a home of the Russian tsars.* Next door to this enormous building is the Hermitage, one of the finest art galleries in the world.

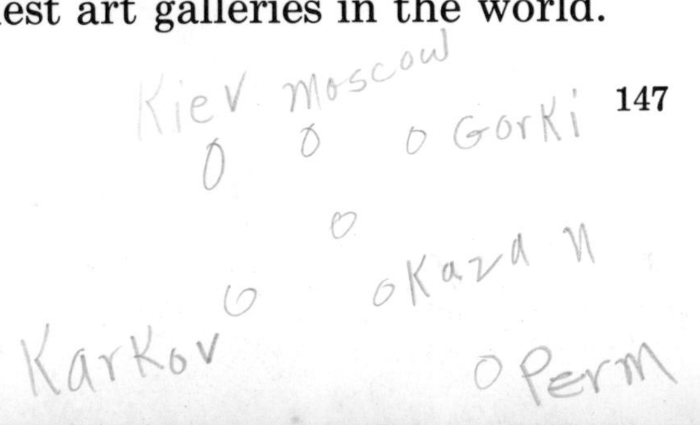

Kiev is the Soviet Union's third largest city. It is more than a thousand years old.

Kiev. We now fly six hundred miles southward to Kiev, the third largest city in the Soviet Union. (See map on page 147.) More than a million people live here. Kiev is located in the Soviet Union's richest farming country, the belt of black soil that stretches through the grassland region. Part of the city stands on a bluff overlooking the Dnieper River. A very old business section called the Podol stretches along the riverbank. As we walk along the wide, tree-lined streets of Kiev, we pass several groups of farm workers. They have come to sell their vegetables in the open market places of the city. We also see many factories, for Kiev is a manufacturing center.

During our stay, we stop to admire the huge wall paintings in the Cathedral of St. Sophia. This is one of the oldest churches in the Soviet Union. There are many other ancient and beautiful buildings here, for Kiev is more than a thousand years old. When it was just a tiny market center, Viking seamen from Scandinavia sailed down the Dnieper River to trade here. Some of them stayed and became the princes of the city. Until about eight hundred years ago, Kiev was the most important city in the country.

Volgograd. Next, we fly eastward to the busy manufacturing city of Volgograd, formerly known as Stalingrad. (See map on

Volgograd was almost completely destroyed during World War II, but has since been rebuilt.

page 147.) This city stretches out in a long line along the Volga River. At first we wonder why Volodia suggested that we come here, for Volgograd, which has a population of 591,000, is much smaller than the other cities we have visited. We understand why when we see a strange monument in the city. This is a roofless, battered building that was damaged in World War II.* It has been left in memory of one of the most important battles of the war. In this battle, the Soviet army and the brave people of the city prevented the German troops from crossing the Volga River and advancing farther into the country. During the struggle, the city was almost completely destroyed, but it has since been rebuilt. We are not surprised to hear that Volgograd is called "City of Heroes."

Tashkent. Last of all, we fly to the southern part of the desert region to visit the city of Tashkent. More than 900,000 people live here. Part of Tashkent has wide streets and modern buildings like the other cities we have seen. Another part, however, is very different. Here the narrow, twisting streets are lined with low, flat-roofed houses made of mud bricks. Instead of church steeples, we see the bright-blue domes of buildings called mosques, where people of the Islamic* faith come to worship. Men in long robes guide donkey carts laden with fruit and vegetables to the market place. Some of the women we see wear veils to cover their faces. Volodia tells us that Tashkent is similar to many other towns and cities in the desert region. This part of the country is known as Soviet Central Asia. Its people live much more like people in the neighboring countries of Asia than like the Russians.

New and growing cities. There are many other cities in the Soviet Union. (See map on page 147.) Thirty-five years ago, most of them were just quiet towns. Then the government began to build factories in them. As people flocked in from the country to work in these factories, the towns grew into busy industrial centers. Some Soviet cities are brand new. They have been established by the government near mines and forests in remote parts of the country. Today, almost half of the people in the Soviet Union live in cities.

DO YOU KNOW

1. Use the pictures in this chapter to help you describe four places in Moscow. Find them on the map on page 138.
2. What was Leningrad first named? Who built it, and where is it located?
3. Describe the city of Tashkent.
4. How many Soviet people live in cities? Where are most of these cities located?

Houses in a new Soviet city. Some new cities are being built in the Soviet Union.

Girls selling ice cream in Gorki Park. There are many large parks in Moscow.

CHAPTER THIRTEEN
SPORTS AND RECREATION

A visit to the park. We are strolling down a shady walk in one of Moscow's many parks, the Gorki Park of Culture and Rest. (See map on page 138.) There are many other people here. Since most of the people of Moscow live in tiny, crowded apartments, they like to get outdoors whenever possible.

There are many things to do in the park. In one section we stop to watch boys and girls riding on an enormous Ferris wheel. In another place, two men are quietly and seriously playing chess. This is a favorite game in the Soviet Union, and some of the world's finest chess players are Soviet citizens. Down by the river, several boys are stepping into a rowboat. A group of girls behind us are on their way to the park theater to see a movie. Many of the other people we pass are just walking about or sitting on benches in the shade and reading. The Soviet people spend a great deal of time reading.

Recreation in the city and countryside. There are other places in Moscow where people may spend their leisure time. Many people enjoy going to movies or attending plays, operas, or ballet performances. They like to visit museums and art galleries, too.

Playing games in the park. Many people spend their leisure time in Moscow's fine parks.

The Soviet people also enjoy going out into the country. When the weather is warm, they go fishing and swimming. Families often hike in the woods and spend the day gathering mushrooms. During the long, cold winters, they take sleigh rides or go skiing on snowy slopes. Sometimes they skate on frozen ponds and rivers.

Vacation trips. Like many people in the United States, Soviet workers get at least two weeks of vacation with pay every year.

Skiers. During the long, snowy winters many people ski, ice skate, and go on sleigh rides.

Sun bathers at Sochi. Many Soviet people spend their vacations at resorts on the Black Sea.

Many of them enjoy taking trips at this time. Only a small number of trusted people are given permission by the government to travel to other countries, but there are pleasant vacation spots within the Soviet Union. Along the sunny beaches that border the Black Sea are resorts where many people come to relax and sunbathe. Other vacationers bicycle through the countryside or take long hiking trips. There are also summer camps for children. These camps are operated by Communist youth clubs.

Sports. The Soviet people like sports just as we do. Nearly every factory, farm, and school has teams for different sports. The team game which the Soviet people enjoy watching most is soccer. In this game, players may not touch the ball with their hands. Instead, a player tries to kick it or knock it across the goal with his head, shoulders, arms, or knees. Another favorite game is

Playing volleyball. All sports clubs in the Soviet Union are controlled by the government.

volleyball. Ice hockey, basketball, and lapta, a game somewhat like baseball, are also enjoyed by many people.

The people who play on teams in the Soviet Union usually belong to sports clubs. There is a big difference between these clubs and those in the United States, however. In the Soviet Union, all athletic organizations are controlled by a special department of the government. People are not allowed to form their own clubs. The government organizes clubs wherever it thinks they are needed. It also closes them any time it wants to.

The government uses athletics to make the Soviet people more useful citizens. In their sports clubs, the people are taught to believe that their system of government is good. They are encouraged to learn skills, such as target shooting and parachute jumping, which will make them good fighters in time of war. The government also believes that sports will help the people to develop strong, healthy bodies that will make them better workers in time of peace.

The Soviet government spends a great deal of money on athletics. Thousands of stadiums and playing fields have been built. There are also many large sports festivals, planned by the government, where athletes from different parts of the country come to compete.

Girls training for Olympic tryouts. The government encourages people to take part in athletics.

The Central Lenin Stadium in Moscow. The government has built thousands of stadiums and playing fields.

Let's attend a sports festival in the city of Moscow. The huge stadium where we have just taken our seats is thronged with people. We see row after row of young athletes marching across the playing field. They carry large banners with the words "Undying Loyalty to the Communist Party" written on them. When they march off, two soccer teams run onto the field. The crowd cheers as they begin to play. One team scores a goal, and the watchers release thousands of colored balloons filled with gas. Up they float into the clear summer air.

Soviet athletes compete in the Olympic Games and other sports events all over the world. The government works hard to train athletes to be champions and gives them special privileges which ordinary citizens do not enjoy. When Soviet teams win, the government tells the people it is because their system of government is better than that of other countries. The Communist leaders also hope that athletic victories will help to convince the rest of the world that communism is better than capitalism.*

DO YOU KNOW

1. Why do many Soviet people like to get outdoors whenever possible?
2. Describe the things people may do in Gorki Park during their leisure time.
3. What is a favorite Soviet vacation spot?
4. Name three sports played in the Soviet Union. Explain why the Soviet government is interested in athletics.

A sports festival in Kiev. Good athletes receive many special privileges in the Soviet Union.

An elementary school. Soviet children who live in cities wear uniforms to school.

CHAPTER FOURTEEN
EDUCATION

The bell has just rung in a large, four-storied stone schoolhouse in the city of Moscow. Boys and girls are marching in straight lines up the steps and through the front door. The girls are dressed alike in long-sleeved, brown dresses with big, white collars and black pinafores. The boys are wearing trousers and shirts that look somewhat like soldiers' uniforms. Soviet children who live in cities wear clothes like these to school until they have finished the eighth grade.

We follow the children into the building and down the hall. On our right is the fourth-grade classroom. The boys and girls here are taking their places quickly and quietly on benches behind double desks. There are just thirty-five pupils in the room. To us, their classroom looks a little bare and gloomy. Large, clean blackboards cover much of the walls. At the front of the room we see a picture of Lenin. When the teacher enters the room, the children jump to their feet and stand quietly by their desks until she asks them to be seated. Then they begin their arithmetic lesson.

Soviet boys and girls attend school six days a week. They have long homework assignments.

These children work very hard in school. In addition to arithmetic, they study reading, spelling, writing, science, geography, and history. They also have classes in music, drawing, and physical education. As a part of all their lessons, they are taught to believe in communism and to obey their government without question. Unlike us, these children must go to school on Saturday. They also have long homework assignments to do. In addition, they spend two hours each week helping to clean their schoolroom or playground, or doing other useful kinds of work.

The boys and girls we are visiting use the Russian language in school, but many other Soviet children do not. In parts of the country where another language is spoken, children study their lessons in that language. From the third grade on, they learn Russian in a special class.

Many of the children we see spend most of their time in school because their mothers work. They eat lunch at school and stay in the afternoon to work on hobbies until their parents get home. They are used to being away from their parents, however. When they were babies, they stayed in nurseries while their mothers worked all day. Then they went to kindergarten from the time they were three until they were seven, and old enough for the first grade.

The school we are visiting goes through the eighth grade. The Soviet government has passed a law that Soviet children should complete this much education. After the fourth grade, the pupils begin to learn a foreign language. They also study the writings of some famous authors from other countries. A great deal of their time is spent studying mathematics and science. In addition, the girls learn how to cook and sew, and the boys are taught to mend shoes and do household tasks.

A school print shop. Boys and girls in the Soviet Union may learn job skills in school.

Job-training schools. Many Soviet boys and girls go to work when they finish the eighth grade, but others go on for more schooling. Some enter special schools called technicums, which prepare them for jobs in industry, farming, or some other field. Students who do not attend technicums may learn job skills in special classes given in factories. Many adults also attend these classes. They want to get as much schooling as possible, for they know that the kind of job a person holds in the Soviet Union depends largely on how much education he has.

High schools. Some Soviet students go on to high school for three years when they finish the eighth grade. There they take subjects that prepare them for the university. In addition, they spend a third of their time learning a trade at a factory or on a farm. The government feels that they should have this experience, even though many of them do not plan to do this kind of work when they become men and women. Students who start working after they complete the eighth grade may take the classes they need for a high school diploma in night school or in correspondence courses.

A chemistry class. Soviet high school students study subjects that prepare them for the university.

Moscow State University. The Soviet Union has about forty universities and many colleges.

Universities and colleges. Only about a third as many students in the Soviet Union attend colleges and universities as in the United States. There are about forty universities and many colleges, called institutes, where students may study engineering, medicine, or other professions. However, these are not enough for all the people who would like to go on to school. Young people must take examinations to enter, and only a few are admitted. Those who are admitted do not have to pay for their education, and many receive money from the government if their grades are good enough. However, while they are in school, they have to spend part of their time working in factories, on farms, or doing other useful work. When they graduate, the government tells them where to work.

In a government boarding school, children are taught to be loyal Communists.

Special schools. There are other kinds of schools in the Soviet Union besides the ones about which we have learned. Young people who are deaf or blind attend schools of their own. Boys and girls with outstanding talent in music, art, or ballet attend schools where they receive special training in addition to their ordinary schoolwork. There are also some boarding schools in the Soviet Union. Many of these are attended by children who come from lonely, remote parts of the country. The government plans to build more boarding schools for children in the cities and towns. The Communists do not want children to live at home, because their parents might teach them about religion or other matters of which the government does not approve. These special schools are supported by the government, like all the other schools and universities in the Soviet Union.

Clubs that teach children to be loyal Communists. Children in the Soviet Union receive a very important part of their education outside of school. The Communist Party has organized clubs for young people of different ages in order to teach them to be loyal to communism. Children belong to an organization called the Little Octobrists until they are nine, and old enough to become Young Pioneers. In these clubs, they go on nature hikes, put on plays, or take part in activities like working in the school garden. They are also taught to believe that communism is good.

A camp for Young Pioneers. Children in Communist youth clubs go on hikes and work on hobbies.

At the age of fourteen, a young person is old enough to join the Komsomols. Before he may do so, however, a member of the Communist Party or two Komsomol members must recommend him. Once he becomes a member, he is expected to behave well, to obey orders, and to study carefully the teachings of communism. If he does all these things, he may become a member of the Communist Party when he is old enough.

DO YOU KNOW

1. Use the pictures in this chapter to describe a Soviet elementary school. What subjects do the children study?
2. What kind of job-training schools may students enter after the eighth grade?
3. How do high school students in the Soviet Union spend a third of their time?
4. Explain what the Young Pioneers are.

Young Pioneers on parade. Communist youth clubs teach children to believe in communism.

An opera house in Leningrad. Russian composers have written operas and other fine musical works.

CHAPTER FIFTEEN

ARTS OF THE PAST

The sound of ringing bells and stirring music fills the beautiful Bolshoi Theater in the city of Moscow tonight. From our seats in the third row, we watch a procession of singers dressed as princes and noblemen march solemnly across the stage. Behind them kneels a great throng of men and women who are playing the part of ordinary townspeople. Suddenly a man in kingly robes appears in the doorway of a church at the center of the stage. "Long live King Boris!" sing the townspeople. "Glory to King Boris!"

The musical play, or opera, that we are watching is *Boris Godunov,* the story of an early Russian ruler. It was composed by Musorgski, a great Russian musician who lived in the nineteenth century, when the Soviet Union was known as Russia. It is only one of the many fine musical works which Russia's composers gave to the world in times gone by.

We listen to some of these musical compositions on our record player after we go home from the opera. First we hear a simple, lovely piece called *Kamarinskaya,* by the nineteenth-century composer Glinka. In several places, the music makes us feel like skipping or tapping our feet. The lively melodies in this composition were borrowed from old Russian folk songs. In his music, Glinka used many of the old folk tunes he had heard as a child.

The next selection we play is wild and lively in some parts and dreamy in others. It makes us think of dark-haired girls stamping and circling in a tribal dance and stopping to rest in the moonlight. This composition is called *Dances of the Polovetsian Maidens.* The nineteenth-century musician Borodin, who wrote it, composed several musical pictures of the people and countryside of Russia.

We feel almost as though we were in church when we listen to our next record. It is the *Russian Easter Overture* by Rimski-Korsakov, who also lived in the nineteenth century. The melody at the beginning is taken from one of the many beautiful hymns which were sung in the Russian Orthodox Church. Rimski-Korsakov based some of his other music on old Russian folk tunes and stories. Maybe you have heard about his beautiful opera *The Snow Maiden.*

An international music competition is held in Moscow, in honor of the Russian composer Tchaikovsky.

How sad and haunting our last record sounds! It is the opening part of a great symphony* called the *Pathétique*. The man who wrote this symphony is Tchaikovsky, Russia's best-loved nineteenth-century composer. Some of Tchaikovsky's music is light and gay, like his mischievous *Nutcracker Suite*. Much of it is thoughtful and tender, however. Although he had enough money to live on and success in his work, he was not a happy person.

Ballet. Some Russian composers wrote beautiful music for the ballet. Imagine that we are watching a performance of Tchaikovsky's ballet *Swan Lake*. Before us on the stage, we see a cool,

A scene from "Swan Lake." The music for this famous ballet was written by Tchaikovsky.

green lake deep in a forest. Girls in filmy, snow-white dresses are dancing on its shores. They are enchanted maidens who change into swans at dawn each day. A young prince has promised to break this spell by giving their queen his undying love. The dancers never say a word. Their graceful movements tell the whole story.

Dancers from Italy and other European countries taught the Russians about ballet in the eighteenth century. The Russians became better than their teachers, however, and improved this art in many ways. Some of the world's greatest dancers have been Russians. Among these are Pavlova, Nijinsky, and Ulanova.

Literature. The works of Russia's writers are as well known as Russian music and ballet. Some Russian literature is very old, and we do not know who wrote it. When we visit the Lenin Library in Moscow, we find a book of old poems about the deeds of ancient heroes. These poems, called byliny, were sung for many years before they were written down. We also find a long story-poem called *The Campaign of Igor* that was written by an unknown author. It tells about a brave warrior who lived in the twelfth century. On a shelf close by is a book of beautiful fairy tales that Russian grandparents have been telling to their grandchildren for many years.

Shelf after shelf in the library is filled with the works of great writers who lived in Russia during the nineteenth century. We pick up a book of poems by Pushkin, one of the best known of these

A statue of Pushkin in Moscow. The Russian poet Pushkin lived in the nineteenth century.

men. Although this great writer also produced stories, he is remembered most for his poetry. The story of the opera *Boris Godunov* was taken from one of his poems.

Now we look at a very thick book called *War and Peace.* You will want to read it sometime. It will make you feel almost as though you were living in Russia in 1812 during a terrible war between France and Russia. The man who wrote this book hated war and anything else that caused people to suffer. He was Tolstoi, one of Russia's greatest writers. Tolstoi was a wealthy nobleman. In his youth he lived a gay, selfish life. As he grew older, however, he became deeply concerned with helping unfortunate people. Finally, he gave up his great wealth and lived among the poor as a simple farmer and shoemaker.

A scene from Tolstoi's novel "War and Peace." Tolstoi was one of Russia's greatest writers.

Studying acting. A Russian director, Stanislavski, helped to make plays more lifelike.

We wish we had time to look through the books of Gogol, Turgenev, Dostoevski, and other great Russian writers. They, too, were often concerned about people who were poor and unhappy. The works of these great writers have helped men and women throughout the world to become more aware of people's problems and the need for solving them.

The theater. Some of Russia's nineteenth-century writers are remembered most for their plays. Two of these men are Ostrovski and Chekhov. The plays they wrote were usually about ordinary people like those the playwrights met in their everyday lives.

Russia gave more than fine plays to the theater, however. During the nineteenth century, many actors played their parts in an unnatural, exaggerated way. A Russian actor and director named

The Hermitage, a museum in Leningrad, contains some of the world's finest art.

Stanislavski thought that it would be better if plays were presented in a natural, true-to-life manner. In 1898, he started the Moscow Art Theater and tried out his ideas. Stanislavski's method of acting is still used by some actors in the United States today.

Architecture. We may see many palaces, churches, and fortresses in the Soviet Union. The most famous fortress, the Kremlin in Moscow, is described on page 142. Many of the palaces, like the stately Winter Palace in Leningrad, were designed by foreign architects. Some of the old churches look somewhat like log cabins with very steep roofs. Others are made of stone or stucco* and have towers topped by spires or domes.

Painting. Inside the churches we visit are beautiful paintings of Mary and Jesus, and of saints. These pictures, called icons, usually contain only one or two figures. Some of them were produced hundreds of years ago.

We see other Russian paintings when we tour the Tretyakov Gallery in Moscow. The work of Russia's best-known painter, Repin, is especially interesting. Like some of the Russian music and literature we have learned about, his paintings often show scenes from his country's history.

DO YOU KNOW

1. Name four Russian composers mentioned in this chapter and read about them in the glossary. Tell about their music.
2. Who taught the Russians about ballet? Describe what you would see if you attended the ballet "Swan Lake."
3. Who was Tolstoi, and what was he like?
4. Explain what an icon is.

Religious pictures called icons are found in churches, museums, and some Soviet homes.

A prize-winning Soviet painting. This picture, called "Grain," won a government prize.

CHAPTER SIXTEEN

ART TODAY IN THE SOVIET UNION

A cold, drizzling rain is falling, but the young man standing on the steps of an art school in Moscow does not seem to notice. His shoulders are slumped forward, and he is staring straight ahead. We ask him, "What is the matter?" but he does not seem to hear. The second time we repeat the question, he finally looks at us and answers slowly, "I've been expelled from school."

"What for?" we ask in surprise.

"Because I painted pictures from my imagination to show how I sometimes feel, instead of the kind the government wanted."

"You mean the government here decides what kind of pictures artists should paint?" we exclaim.

"Yes. It also decides what kind of music and books composers and authors should write," he replies.

A painter. The government wants pictures that encourage people to be patriotic and to work hard.

Why is the government interested in art? The next day we ask a man at the American Embassy why the government wants to control art in the Soviet Union.

"The Soviet leaders believe that art should be used to teach people to be loyal Communists," he explains. "For this reason, they encourage only the kind of art that praises the Soviet Union or inspires people to work hard for their country. Of course, they forbid all art that criticizes communism or shows that people in other countries are happier than the Soviet people."

The Tretyakov Gallery in Moscow. People are encouraged to enjoy government-approved art.

Shostakovich. One of his symphonies honors the people of Leningrad who fought in World War II.

Some examples of art the Soviet leaders like. The embassy official shows us some paintings, records, and books the Soviet leaders approve. First we look at a picture called "Grain" by the Soviet painter Yablonskaya. It looks almost like a poster advertising life on a Communist collective farm. Next we listen to the *Leningrad Symphony* by the well-known Soviet composer Shostakovich. The music in this composition describes the way the people of Leningrad resisted the German army in World War II. Then we glance through some books by the Soviet writers Gorki and Sholokhov. The heroes in these novels are proud to live under a Communist government.

What happens to artists who displease the government? Artists who do not produce works like the ones we saw have a very hard time in the Soviet Union. The young man we saw at the art school will not be permitted to continue his education because he wanted to paint in his own way. Recently, the Soviet writer Pasternak was not allowed to have his novel *Doctor Zhivago* published in the Soviet Union because it showed that the Communist Revolution did not bring a happier way of life to the Soviet people. Pasternak sent it to Italy, where it was published. The Nobel* prize for literature was awarded to him for writing this book, but the Soviet leaders were so angry they would not permit him to accept it.

Sometimes the leaders do not decide they disapprove of an artist's work until after it has been made public. When this happens, the artist is told to apologize in public for producing it. If he does not, his music may no longer be heard or his books may not be printed.

How does the government encourage the kind of art it likes? The Soviet leaders work just as hard to encourage the kind of art they like as they do to prevent the kind they do not like. As long as writers, painters, dancers, and musicians do as they are told, the government pays them high salaries and furnishes them with better apartments than ordinary workers have. There are also fine government-supported schools where children with artistic talents may study art, music, and ballet. Of course, these students must be careful not to displease the government or they will be expelled.

The government also spends a great deal of money bringing the kind of art it likes to the Soviet people. There are hundreds of fine

Sholokhov has written several novels describing life under communism in the Soviet Union.

public art galleries, museums, and libraries in the country. Books are published by government-owned publishing houses, and cost very little money. Since theaters and orchestras are supported by the government, tickets to plays and concerts are very inexpensive and most people can afford to go.

Much money is also spent bringing Soviet art to people in other countries. The nation's finest dancers and musicians are sent to perform in foreign lands. Perhaps you heard the pianist Emil Gilels or saw the Moiseyev dance group when they were in the United States. The Soviet leaders hope that people in other countries who attend these beautiful performances will think the Soviet Union is a peaceful country. This will make them forget that it really plans to dominate the world some day.

DO YOU KNOW

1. Explain why the Soviet government wants to control art in the Soviet Union.
2. Give some examples of music and painting that are approved by the government.
3. What happens to people who produce the kind of art the government does not want?
4. Tell how the government encourages the kind of art it wants.

The Moiseyev folk dancers toured the United States. The Soviet Union sends many artists abroad.

GLOSSARY

Your study of the Soviet Union will be more interesting if you take time to use this glossary. You should turn to this glossary each time a word that you read in the text is marked with an asterisk (*), unless you clearly understand the word. The names of people and places in the Soviet Union which are mentioned in the book have also been included in this glossary. The letters that appear inside the brackets following each word show you how the word should sound when it is correctly pronounced. The capital letters used to indicate the pronunciation show you which syllable of the word is to receive the chief stress, as: **Baku** *(bah KOO)*.

The meaning of each word in the glossary is explained to help you understand the text and pictures of this book. You will learn much more about the Soviet Union if you will use this glossary.

Alexander II, 1818-1881. Ruler of Russia from 1855 to 1881. Freed the serfs and made other reforms. Was assassinated by a secret revolutionary group.

allies *(uh LIZ).* Nations that have joined together for better protection against an enemy.

Angara *(un gu RA)* **River.** A river in the eastern part of the Soviet Union. Flows from the southwestern part of Lake Baikal to the Yenisei River. (See map, page 132.)

Antarctic. Refers to the parts of the Pacific, Atlantic, and Indian oceans which border the continent of Antarctica. Also refers to Antarctica.

Aral *(AR uhl)* **Sea.** A shallow, inland sea in the southern part of the Soviet Union. (See map, page 10.)

Arctic Circle. An imaginary line around the earth, about 1,600 miles south of the North Pole.

Baikal *(bi KAL),* **Lake.** The deepest lake in the world. Located in the southeastern part of the Soviet Union. (See map, page 11.)

Baku *(bah KOO).* A port city on the Caspian Sea. (See map, page 10.) Located in one of the Soviet Union's main oil-producing areas.

Balkhash *(bahl KAHSH),* **Lake.** A narrow, shallow lake in the south central part of the Soviet Union. (See map, page 10.)

Baltic *(BAWL tihk)* **Sea.** A large sea located in northern Europe. It forms part of the western border of the Soviet Union. (See map, page 10.)

Barents *(BAR uhnts)* **Sea.** Part of the Arctic Ocean. Borders the Soviet Union on the northwest. (See map, page 10.)

Belaya *(BYEH luh yuh)* **River.** A river in the western part of the Soviet Union. Begins in the Ural Mountains. (See map, page 10.)

Bering Sea. Section of the Pacific Ocean located between the Soviet Union and Alaska. (See map, page 11.)

Black Sea. A large body of water located between the Soviet Union and Turkey. (See map, page 10.)

Bolshevik *(BAHL shuh vihk)* **Party.** A group of people in Russia who believed that Communist governments should be established throughout the world by revolution. The Bolsheviks (or Communists) gained control of the Russian government in 1917.

Borodin *(buh ruh DYEEN),* **Aleksandr Porfirevich,** 1834-1887. A Russian doctor and professor of chemistry who spent much of his leisure time studying and writing music.

borsch *(BAWRSH).* A Russian soup that is colored with the juice of red beets.

Bosporus *(BAHS po ruhs).* A narrow waterway leading out of the southwestern end of the Black Sea.

capitalism. A system in which individual people or private corporations own land, factories, and other property used for making a living.

Caspian *(KAS pih uhn)* **Sea.** A salty, inland body of water located between the Soviet Union and Iran. (See map, page 10.)

Catherine II, 1729-1796, called **Catherine the Great.** A German princess who married the heir to the Russian throne when she was sixteen. Forced him from the throne in 1762 and became the nation's ruler.

Caucasus *(KAW kuh suhs)* **Mountains.** A mountain range in the southern part of the Soviet Union, between the Black and Caspian seas. (See map, page 10.)

censor. To examine materials such as books and magazines before printing to remove anything considered harmful.

Chekhov *(CHEH kawf),* **Anton Pavlovich,** 1860-1904. A Russian playwright and short-story writer.

chromium *(KRO mih uhm).* A grayish-colored metal that does not rust easily. Used to make stainless steel. Also used to coat, or plate, automobile parts and other metal articles.

coal tar. A sticky material obtained from coal. Used to make dyes and medicines.

coke. A fuel made by heating soft coal until it loses some of its gases. Used in blast furnaces to smelt iron ore.

combine *(KAHM bin).* A machine that cuts, threshes, and cleans grain while moving across a field.

communism. A term used to describe a way of living in which all land and other property is owned by the community. Also refers to the teachings and actions of the Soviet Communist Party and of the Communist parties in other countries. (See pages 8, 9, and 56-67.)

Communist Revolution. The revolution of November, 1917, which brought the Communists to power in Russia.

Constantinople *(kahn stan tih NO puhl).* The former name of the city of Istanbul, which is located on the Bosporus in Turkey. See **Bosporus.**

Crimea *(kri MEE uh).* A peninsula of the Soviet Union, extending into the Black Sea. (See map, page 10.)

Crimean *(kri MEE uhn)* **War,** 1854-1856. A war in which Russia was defeated by France, England, Sardinia, and Turkey.

Cyrillic *(sih RIHL ihk)* **alphabet.** The alphabet used in writing Russian.

Dardanelles *(dahr duh NELZ).* One of the narrow water passages between the Black and Mediterranean seas.

dictator. A ruler who has complete power over his people.

Dnieper *(NEE puhr)* **River.** Third largest river in Europe. Flows through the western part of the Soviet Union and into the Black Sea. (See map, page 132.)

Donets *(do NETS)* **Basin.** One of the main coal-producing regions of the Soviet Union. Located near the Black Sea.

Don River. A river in the western part of the Soviet Union. It flows into the Sea of Azov, an arm of the Black Sea. (See map, page 10.)

Dostoevski *(dahs tuh YEV skih),* **Fëdor Mikhailovich,** 1821-1881. A Russian novelist whose writing shows deep understanding of the way people think.

ermine *(UHR mihn).* A small animal of the weasel family that lives in northern regions. Its fur becomes white in winter except for the tip of its tail, which remains black.

Estonia *(es TO nih uh).* A small European country which was forced to become a part of the Soviet Union in 1940. The Soviet government considers it to be a republic of the Soviet Union. (See map, page 61.) The United States does not recognize this action.

Finland, Gulf of. An arm of the Baltic Sea. Located between the Soviet Union and Finland. (See map, page 10.)

Gilels, Emil, 1916- . One of three Soviet pianists to have the title "People's Artist of the U.S.S.R."

Glinka *(GLIHNG kuh),* **Mikhail Ivanovich,** 1803-1857. A Russian composer who wrote musical works based on Russian folk songs. He is considered the founder of Russian national music.

Gogol *(GAW gawl),* **Nikolai Vasilievich,** 1809-1852. A Russian playwright and novelist.

Gorki *(GAWR kih),* **Maksim,** 1868-1936. Russian novelist who became a strong supporter of communism.

Greater Moscow. Includes the city of Moscow and its suburbs.

hydroelectricity *(hi dro ee lek TRIHS uh tih).* Electricity produced by water power. Water held back by a dam is allowed to flow through openings in the dam. The force of the rushing water turns generators to produce electricity.

Ili *(EE LEE)* **River.** A river that flows from northwestern China into Lake Balkhash in the southern part of the Soviet Union. (See map, page 10.)

Indian Ocean. A large body of water that lies south of India. It stretches west as far as Africa and east as far as Australia.

Islamic *(ihs LAM ihk)* **faith,** or **Islam.** The religion founded by an Arabian prophet named Mohammed.

Ivan IV, 1530-1584, called **Ivan the Terrible.** The first Russian ruler to be crowned tsar. See **tsar.**

Ivanovo *(ih VA nuh vuh).* A manufacturing city in the western part of the Soviet Union. (See map, page 147.)

Japan, Sea of. The part of the Pacific Ocean that borders the Soviet Union on the southeast. (See map, page 11.)

Karaganda *(kah rah gahn DAH).* A city in one of the Soviet Union's largest coal-mining regions. (See map, page 106.)

Kazakh *(kah ZAHK)* **S.S.R.** A republic of the Soviet Union. (See map, page 61.)

Khrushchev *(kroosh CHAWF),* **Nikita Sergeevich,** 1894- . Head of both the Communist Party and the government of the Soviet Union. As a young man worked as a shepherd and factory laborer. Joined the Communist Party in 1918. Overcame his rivals to become the Party leader after Stalin's death.

Kiev *(KEE ef).* Third largest city in the Soviet Union. Located on the Dnieper River in the western part of the country. (See map, page 10.) Was the capital of Kievan Russia. See **Kievan Russia.**

Kievan *(kee EV uhn)* **Russia.** The Slavic nation which was established along the banks of the Dnieper River in the 9th century. Its capital was Kiev. (See map, page 34.) See **Slavic.**

Kremlin *(KREM lihn).* Walled fortress in the heart of Moscow. (See map, page 138.) It is the seat of the Soviet Union's government.

Krivoi Rog *(KRIHV oi ROG).* A city in Ukrainian S.S.R. Located in a rich iron-mining region. (See map, page 109.)

Kuznetsk *(kooz NETSK)* **Basin.** Region in central Siberia where vast coal deposits are located. (See map, page 106.)

Latvia *(LAT vih uh).* A small European country which was forced to become a part of the Soviet Union in 1940. The Soviet government considers it to be a republic of the Soviet Union. (See map, page 61.) The United States does not recognize this action.

Lena *(LEE nuh)* **River.** The longest river in the Soviet Union. It begins near Lake Baikal and flows to the Arctic Ocean. (See map, page 11.)

Lenin *(LEN ihn),* 1870-1924. Real name was Vladimir Ilich Ulyanov. Spent most of his young manhood working to overthrow the Russian government. Led the Communist Revolution of November, 1917, and became the leader of the new government. Is called the founder of the Soviet Union.

Leningrad *(LEN ihn grad).* Second largest city in the Soviet Union. Located on the Neva River where it flows into the Gulf of Finland. (See map, page 10.) Founded by Peter the Great. Was called St. Petersburg until 1914, when its name was changed to Petrograd. After Lenin's death, it was named Leningrad.

lichens *(LI kuhnz).* Very small, tough plants that can grow in almost any climate. They look like moss and are often seen on rocks and old stumps.

Lithuania *(lith u AY nih uh).* A small European country which was forced to become a part of the Soviet Union in 1940. The Soviet government considers it to be a republic of the Soviet Union. (See map, page 61.) The United States does not recognize this action.

Magnitogorsk *(mag NEE to gawrsk).* A city in the southern part of the Ural Mountains. Is the Soviet Union's main iron and steel center. (See map, page 120.)

Marx, Karl, 1818-1883. A German thinker who believed that the working-class people throughout the world would unite to overthrow their old governments and replace them with communism. See **communism.** He is sometimes called the father of modern communism. Was exiled from Germany for his revolutionary activities and spent his last years in England.

Mediterranean *(med uh tuh RAY nee uhn)* **Sea.** An inland sea bounded by Europe, Asia, and Africa.

Moiseyev *(moi SAY yef)* **dance group.** A Soviet folk dance company established in 1937. It has toured 27 countries.

Mongols *(MAHNG guhlz).* People from the vast territory called Mongolia, which lies north of China.

Moscow *(MAHS kau).* The capital and largest city of the Soviet Union. (See maps, pages 10 and 138.)

Moskva *(mus KVA)* **River.** A short river in the western part of the Soviet Union. Flows through the city of Moscow. (See maps, pages 132 and 138.)

mosque *(MAHSK).* A place of worship for people of the Islamic faith. See **Islamic faith.**

Murmansk *(moor MANSK).* The only port in the northern part of the Soviet Union whose harbor does not freeze in winter. Its climate is influenced by a warm ocean current called the North Atlantic Drift. An important fishing center. (See map, page 147.)

Musorgski *(moo SAWRG skih),* **Modest Petrovich,** 1835-1881. A Russian composer who earned his living as a government clerk. Wrote operas, songs, and other musical works.

Napoleon *(nuh POE lee uhn)* **Bonaparte,** 1769-1821. A French general. Became emperor of France in 1804. Conquered most of Europe, but was defeated by combined European armies. Died in exile.

Neva *(NEE vuh)* **River.** A short river near the western border of the Soviet Union. Flows into the Gulf of Finland. (See map, page 132.)

Nicholas II, 1868-1918. The last of the tsars to rule Russia. Was forced to leave his throne by the revolution of March, 1917.

Nijinsky *(nih ZHIN skih),* **Waslaw,** 1890-1950. A Russian ballet dancer. He was considered to be one of the world's greatest dancers.

Nobel *(no BEL)* **prize.** One of five annual prizes given for outstanding contributions in the fields of science, literature, and peace. The money for the Nobel prizes was willed by the Swedish inventor Alfred Nobel.

oases *(o AY seez).* Fertile areas in a desert where there is enough water to permit vegetation to grow.

Ob *(AWB)* **River.** A long river in the west central part of the Soviet Union. Flows into the Gulf of Ob, which leads into the Arctic Ocean. (See map, page 10.)

Oka *(uh KA)* **River.** A river in the western part of the Soviet Union. Flows into the Volga River. (See map, page 132.)

Okhotsk *(o KAHTSK),* **Sea of.** An arm of the Pacific Ocean. Located off the central part of the Soviet Union's east coast. (See map, page 11.)

Olympic Games. A series of contests held every four years, in which the best amateur athletes from many countries compete.

Orthodox Eastern Church. The name given to the main family of Christian churches in eastern Europe, Asia, and Egypt. This group of churches separated from the Roman Catholic Church in 1054.

Ostrovski *(ahs TRAHF skih),* **Aleksandr Nikolaevich,** 1823-1886. A Russian writer of plays, mainly comedies.

Pasternak *(pah stuhr NAK),* **Boris Leonidovich,** 1890-1960. A Russian poet. Author of the book **Doctor Zhivago.**

Pavlova *(PA vluh vuh),* **Anna,** 1885-1931. A famous Russian ballet dancer.

peasant. In Europe, a person who owns a small farm or works as a farm laborer.

Persia. Former name of the country of Iran, which is located in the southwestern part of Asia.

Peter I, 1672-1725, called **Peter the Great.** A powerful Russian tsar who often used brutal methods to bring modern ways to his country. He founded the city of St. Petersburg, now called Leningrad.

Petrograd *(PET roe grad).* Name given to the city of St. Petersburg in 1914. In 1924 the city's name was changed to Leningrad. See **Leningrad.**

phosphate *(FAHS fayt).* A mineral product found in bones and certain rocks. Used in making fertilizers.

Pushkin *(POOSH kihn),* **Aleksander Sergeevich,** 1799-1827. A playwright and poet. The first Russian to write in a realistic, simple manner instead of copying the French writers of his time. Is called the father of modern Russian literature.

Repin *(RYAY pyihn),* **Ilya Efimovich,** 1844-1930. A Russian artist who painted many scenes from Russian history.

Rimski-Korsakov *(RIM skih KAWR suh kawf),* **Nikolai Andreevich,** 1844-1908. A Russian naval officer who resigned and became a professor of music and a composer. Wrote symphonies, operas, piano compositions, and other musical works.

Romanov *(RO muh nawf),* **Michael,** 1596-1645. Was elected by an assembly of the people to be tsar of Russia in 1613. His descendants ruled the country until the revolution of March, 1917. See **tsar.**

Rules of the Communist Party of the Soviet Union. A document, much like a constitution, explaining what the Soviet Communist Party is, how it is organized, and what the duties of its members are.

Russia. Name often used when referring to the Soviet Union. Was the official name of the country until December, 1922. Also refers to the largest republic in the Soviet Union, the Russian Soviet Federated Socialist Republic. (See map, page 61.)

Russian. The name of the largest group of people in the Soviet Union. (See map, page 69.) Also the official language of the country.

Russian Orthodox Church. The official church of Russia before the Communist Revolution. One of the Orthodox Eastern family of churches. See **Orthodox Eastern.**

sable. A small, dark-brown animal of the weasel family.

Saint Petersburg. Original name for the city of Leningrad. See **Leningrad.**

Samarkand *(SAM uhr kand).* One of the oldest cities in the Soviet Union. Located in central Uzbek S.S.R. (See map, page 147.)

samovar *(SAM o vahr).* A metal vessel used to heat water for tea. Has a pipe rising through the center. A small charcoal fire in the pipe heats the water.

Saratov *(su RA tuhf).* A manufacturing city located on the banks of the Volga River, in the western part of the Soviet Union. (See map, page 147.)

satellite. In the study of astronomy, refers to a smaller body, such as the moon, which revolves around a larger body, such as the earth.

Scandinavia *(skan duh NAY vih uh).* Refers to the part of northern Europe that includes the countries of Norway, Sweden, Denmark, Iceland, and other nearby islands.

serf. A person who is somewhat like a slave. He is not allowed to leave the land on which he works.

Sholokhov *(SHAW luh kawf),* **Mikhail Aleksandrovich,** 1905- . A Soviet novelist.

Shostakovich *(shahs tuh KO vihch),* **Dimitri Dimitrievich,** 1906- . A Soviet composer.

Siberia *(si BEER ih uh).* The northern part of Asia that stretches from the Ural Mountains to the Pacific Ocean.

Slavic *(SLAHV ihk).* Refers to the Slavs and to their language. See **Slavs.**

Slavs *(SLAHVZ).* A large group of people who speak languages that are somewhat the same. They are descendants of the early Slavs who were living near the western borders of the Soviet Union when Christ was born. Russians, Poles, and Bulgarians all belong to the Slavic group of people.

smelt. To melt ore in order to separate the metal from the waste materials.

Sochi *(SAW chih).* A port and resort city on the northeastern coast of the Black Sea.

Soviet Central Asia. The name given to the part of the Soviet Union which includes the Turkmen, Kirghiz, Tadzhik, and Uzbek republics. Some people also include the republic of Kazakh in this region. (See map, page 61.)

Stalin *(STAH lihn),* **Joseph,** 1879-1953. Real name was Iosif Vissarionovich Dzhugashvili. Was the son of a shoemaker in Georgian S.S.R. (See map, page 61.) Before the Communist Revolution, he was exiled many times for working against the government. After Lenin's death, he overcame other rivals to become the dictator of the Soviet Union. See **Lenin** and **dictator.**

Stanislavski *(stan ih SLAF skih),* 1863-1938. Real name was Konstantin Sergeevich Alekseev. A Russian actor and producer of plays.

steppe *(STEP).* A vast plain that is flat and usually grassy and treeless.

stucco. A material such as plaster used to coat walls.

sulfur. A yellow element which gives off a rotten-egg odor when melted or rubbed. Is found combined with other elements or by itself. Used in making insect killers, fertilizers, medicines, paper, and many other products.

symphony *(SIHM foe nih).* A musical composition played by a full orchestra. Usually has three or four parts, or movements.

taiga *(TI guh).* The vast evergreen forest of the Soviet Union.

Tashkent *(tash KENT).* The capital of Uzbek S.S.R. and the largest city in Soviet Central Asia. See **Soviet Central Asia.** (See maps, pages 61 and 147.)

Tchaikovsky *(chi KAWF skih),* **Pëtr Ilich,** 1840-1893. A Russian composer. Wrote symphonies, ballets, operas, and other types of musical works.

Tolstoi *(tahl STOI),* **Count Nikolaevich,** 1828-1910. A Russian nobleman who became a great novelist and a religious thinker.

Transcaucasia *(trans kaw KAY zhuh).* The part of the Soviet Union which lies south of the Caucasus Mountains.

tsar *(ZAHR).* The title used by the rulers of Russia from the sixteenth century to the revolution of March, 1917.

tundra *(TOON druh).* The cold, treeless plains which are located around the Arctic Ocean.

tungsten *(TUNG stuhn).* A rare metallic element that is silver-white in color and very hard. Is used in making high-quality steel, wires for electric light bulbs, and other products.

turbine. An engine run by the force of rushing water striking against blades fitted on a driveshaft. Used to drive electric generators.

Turgenev *(toor GAY nyuhf),* **Ivan Sergeevich,** 1818-1883. A Russian novelist.

Turkic *(TUHR kihk).* Refers to the tribesmen who were living in the desert region of the Soviet Union more than a thousand years ago. Also refers to their descendants.

Ukraine *(yu KRAYN).* Refers to Ukrainian S.S.R., a republic of the Soviet Union, located in the southwestern part of the country. (See map, page 61.)

Ulanova, Galina, 1908- . A Soviet ballerina. Has been awarded the title of "People's Artist of the U.S.S.R."

Ural *(YUR uhl)* **Mountains.** The mountain system in the Soviet Union which is considered to be the boundary between Europe and Asia. (See map, pages 10 and 11.)

Uzbek *(OOZ bek).* Refers to Uzbek S.S.R., a republic of the Soviet Union, located in the southern part of the country. (See map, page 61.) Also refers to the people of this republic.

Vikings *(VI kings).* Daring Scandinavian warriors who raided the coasts of Europe from about 800 to 1050 A. D.

Vladivostok *(vlad uh vuhs TAHK).* A seaport on the Pacific coast of the Soviet Union. (See map, page 147.)

Volga *(VAHL guh)* **River.** Longest river in Europe. It flows through the western part of the Soviet Union to the Caspian Sea. (See map, page 10.)

Volgograd *(VAHL guh grad).* A city located on the Volga River in the western part of the Soviet Union. (See map, page 147.)

wagon-lit *(va gawn LEE).* A railroad car equipped for sleeping.

White Sea. A gulf of the Barents Sea, which borders the Soviet Union on the northwest. (See map, page 10.)

World War I, 1914-1919. The first war in history which involved nearly every part of the world. The Central Powers — Germany, Austria, Turkey, and Bulgaria — were defeated by the Allies. These included Great Britain, France, Russia, Japan, and the United States.

World War II, 1939-1945. The second war in history which involved nearly every part of the world. The Allied Powers, which included the United States, Great Britain, the Soviet Union, France, and many other countries, defeated the Axis Powers. These included mainly Germany, Italy, and Japan. The Soviet Union, the United States, and Japan did not enter World War II until 1941.

Yablonskaya *(yah BLAWN ski yuh),* **Tatyana Nilovna,** 1917- . A Soviet painter.

Yenisei *(yen uh SAY)* **River.** A long river which flows through the central part of the Soviet Union to the Gulf of Yenisei on the Arctic coast. (See map, page 11.)

Index

(Page numbers in this Index that are preceded by *"p."* refer to pictures.)

agriculture, 83-94, 95-103; *p.* 12, 19, 20, 29, 83, 85, 86, 88-90, 93, 94, 97, 99, 101; *maps* 87, 91, 92
airplanes, 134; *p.* 135
Alaska, 41
Alexander II, 43; *p.* 43
architecture, 176; *p.* 131, 139-142, 145, 165
Armenians, 75; *p.* 75
arts, 169-184; *p.* 39, 169, 171-181, 183, 184
  of the past, 169-177; *p.* 169, 171-177
  of today, 178-184; *p.* 178-181, 183, 184
automobiles, 131

Baku, 108; *p.* 108
Belorussians, 74; *p.* 74; *map* 69
Black Sea, 22, 31-32; *p.* 22; *map* 13
Bolshevik Party, 48

canals, 133-134; *p.* 133; *map* 132
Catherine the Great, 39-40; *p.* 40
Caucasus Mountains, 21; *p.* 21; *map* 10
Caucasus region, 21-22; *map* 13
Central Siberian Plateau, 17; *map* 11
cities, 108, 109, 137-151; *p.* 131, 137, 139-143, 145, 146, 148, 149, 151; *maps* 138, 147
  Baku, 108; *p.* 108
  Kiev, 35, 148-149; *p.* 36, 148, 159; *maps* 34, 147
  Leningrad, 146-147; *p.* 39, 146; *map* 147
  Magnitogorsk, 109, 119; *map* 147
  Moscow, 36, 41, 49, 134, 137-146; *p.* 131, 137, 139-143, 145, 152, 153, 158; *maps* 138, 147
  new cities, 150-151; *p.* 151
  Samarkand, 77-78; *map* 147
  Tashkent, 150; *map* 147
  Volgograd, 149-150; *p.* 149; *map* 147
climate, 25-33; *p.* 25, 26, 29-33; *map* 28
clothing, 69, 73, 77, 99; *p.* 32, 70-80, 94, 99, 153, 154, 156, 157
coal, 106-107; *p.* 107; *map* 106
collective farms, 84, 95-103
communications, 135-136; *p.* 136
communism, 48, 56-67
Communist Party, 56-60, 65-67
Communists, 48-52, 81, 166-167
constitution, 60-63
courts, 63-64; *p.* 64
Crimea, 32; *p.* 32; *map* 10
Crimean War, 41
crops, 88-89, 91-93; *p.* 88, 89, 93, 94; *maps* 87, 92
Cyrillic alphabet, 70

dancers, 172; *p.* 172, 184
desert region, 23, 30; *p.* 23, 30; *map* 13
Dnieper River, 35; *map* 132
dress. See **clothing.**
Duma, 44, 45

education, 160-168; *p.* 160, 161, 163-168
  schools, 160-167; *p.* 160, 161, 163-166
  youth clubs, 167-168; *p.* 167, 168

farming. See **agriculture.**
farm workers, 43, 84-85, 99; *p.* 42, 99
Fertile Triangle, 87, 88, 91; *p.* 88, 89; *maps* 87, 91, 92
fishing, 112-113; *p.* 113
Five-Year Plans, 52
food, 103, 128; *p.* 101, 103
forest region, 16-19, 27-28; *p.* 15, 16, 19; *map* 13
forests, 111-112, 122

gas, 108-109; *map* 106
Georgians, 75
government, 56-67, 118, 129, 135, 155, 156-157, 158-159, 178-184; *p.* 56-58, 60, 63-67; *map* 61
  elections, 59-60; *p.* 60
grain, 88-89; *p.* 20, 88, 89; *map* 87
grassland region, 20, 29; *p.* 20; *map* 13

highlands, 17
history, 34-55; *p.* 36-40, 42-47, 49-51, 53-55; *map* 34
  early, 34-45, 142-143; *p.* 36-40, 42-45; *map* 34
  modern, 46-55; *p.* 46, 47, 49-51, 53-55
homes, 72, 79, 100, 101-102; *p.* 95, 100, 102, 103, 151
hydroelectricity, 105-106; *p.* 105; *map* 106

icons, 177; *p.* 177
industry, 115-125; *p.* 115, 116, 118, 119, 121-123, 125; *map* 120; *graph* 117
  chemical, 120-122; *p.* 121, 122; *map* 120
  metal, 119-120; *p.* 115, 118, 119, 125; *map* 120
  textile, 123-124; *p.* 123; *map* 120
iron ore, 109; *map* 109
Ivan IV, 36-37; *p.* 37
Ivan the Terrible. See **Ivan IV.**

Khrushchev, Nikita S., 55, 58, 59; *p.* 58, 85
Kiev, 35, 148-149; *p.* 36, 148, 159; *maps* 34, 147
Kievan Russia, 35; *map* 34
Kremlin, 140, 142; *p.* 142; *map* 138

Lake Baikal, 17; *p.* 17; *map* 11
Lake Balkhash, 23; *map* 10
land, 13-24; *p.* 12, 14-24; *map* 13
language, 70, 73, 162; *p.* 70
Lena River, 15; *p.* 15; *map* 132
Lenin, 46-48; *p.* 47
Leningrad, 146-147; *p.* 39, 146, 169; *map* 147
literature, 173-175, 182
livestock, 89-91; *p.* 90; *map* 91

Magnitogorsk, 109, 119; *map* 147
Marx, Karl, 48; *p.* 46
minerals, 106-110; *p.* 104, 107, 108, 110, 111; *maps* 106, 109
Mongols, 35-36; *p.* 36
Moscow, 36, 41, 49, 134, 137-146; *p.* 131, 137, 139-143, 145, 152, 153, 158; *maps* 138, 147
Moskva River, 139; *p.* 137; *maps* 132, 138
mountains, 13, 17, 20, 21, 22, 23-24, 30-31; *p.* 18, 21, 24
music, 169-171, 181; *p.* 169, 171, 172

Napoleon, 40-41
natural resources, 104-114; *p.* 104, 105, 107, 108, 110-114; *maps* 106, 109
Nicholas II, 44, 45; *p.* 45
North Atlantic Drift, 27

oil, 108; *p.* 108; *map* 106

painting, 177, 178-179, 181; *p.* 176, 177, 178-180
Party Presidium, 58, 59
Pasternak, 182
peasants, 43, 51-52; *p.* 42
people, 68-82; *p.* 32, 42, 49, 50, 53, 68, 70-80, 94, 96-99, 101-103, 116, 152-157; *maps* 69, 81
Peter I, 38-39; *p.* 38
Peter the Great. See **Peter I.**
plains, 14-15, 18-19
plateaus, 17
population, 81-82; *map* 81
Pushkin, 173-174; *p.* 173

radio, 135
railroads, 127-130; *p.* 127, 129; *map* 126
rainfall, 28, 29, 30, 31-33; *map* 28
recreation, 72, 73, 152-155; *p.* 75, 152-155
Red Square, 139-140; *p.* 139, 140; *map* 138
reindeer, *p.* 33; *map* 91
religion, 71, 77-78; *p.* 71, 78, 177
revolutions, 43-45, 49-51; *p.* 44, 47, 49
Revolution of 1905, 43-44; *p.* 44
Revolution of March, 1917, 44-45
Revolution of November, 1917, (Communist Revolution), 49; *p.* 49
rivers, 132-134; *p.* 15, 18, 112, 137; *map* 132
roads, 130-131; *p.* 130; *map* 126
Romanov family, 37, 38
Romanov, Michael, 37
Russians, 69-72, 81; *p.* 72; *map* 69

Samarkand, 77-78; *map* 147
schools, 160-167; *p.* 160, 161, 163-166
elementary schools, 160-162; *p.* 160, 161
high schools, 164; *p.* 164
job-training schools, 163; *p.* 163
special schools, 166-167; *p.* 166
universities and colleges, 165; *p.* 165
seas, 14; *map* 10-11
serfs, 42, 43
Sholokhov, 182; *p.* 183
Shostakovich, 181; *p.* 181
Siberia, 28; *p.* 12, 94
size, 13
Slavs, 34-35
sports, 155-159; *p.* 156-159
Stalin, Joseph, 52, 55, 75
Stanislavski, 176
state farms, 84
steppe, 20; *p.* 20

taiga, 16; *p.* 16; *map* 13
Tashkent, 150; *map* 147
Tchaikovsky, 171; *p.* 171
television 135; *p.* 136
theater, 175-176; *p.* 175
Tolstoi, 174
Transcaucasia, 22
transportation, 19, 127-134; *p.* 127, 129-131, 133, 135; *maps* 126, 132, 134
air, 134; *p.* 135; *map* 134
land, 127-131; *p.* 14, 26, 33, 127, 129, 130, 131; *map* 126
water, 132-134; *p.* 133; *map* 132
tribesmen, 78-79
tsars, 36-39, 42-43, 44, 45; *p.* 37, 38, 43, 45
tundra, 14-15, 27; *p.* 14; *map* 13

Ukraine, *p.* 29
Ukrainians, 73; *p.* 73; *map* 69
universities, 146, 165; *p.* 165
Ural Mountains, 13, 18; *p.* 18
Uzbeks, 76-78; *p.* 76, 77

Vikings, 35
villages, 77, 95-103; *p.* 19, 95-103, 130
Volga River, 19, 132-133; *map* 132
Volgograd, 149-150; *p.* 149; *map* 147

water power, 105-106; *p.* 55, 105; *map* 106

youth clubs, 167-168; *p.* 167, 168

LIST OF MAPS

Global Relief 8
Political Relief .... 10 and 11
Geographical Regions 13
Average Annual Rainfall 28
History 34
Republics 61
Peoples 69
Population Per Square Mile 81
Crops: Wheat, Rye, Corn, Millet, Oats, and Barley 87
Livestock: Cattle, Reindeer, Pigs, and Sheep 91
Crops: Sugar Beets, Sunflower Seeds, Potatoes, Cotton, and Linseed 92
Fuels and Power 106
Mineral Resources 109
Industries Graph 117
Industries 120
Main Railroads 126
Highways 126
Rivers and Canals 132
Airways 134
Moscow 138
Cities 147

MOSCOW
AFGHANISTAN
CHINA